To Isabel, Debbie and Kate,
with thanks for your love and
your laughter.

THE CASE AGAINST CHRIST

JOHN YOUNG

Hodder & Stoughton
LONDON SYDNEY AUCKLAND

Copyright © 1986 by John Young. First printed by Hodder and
Stoughton 1986. New material copyright © 1994 by John Young.
This edition 1994.

The right of John Young to be identified as the Author of the Work
has been asserted by him in accordance with the Copyright, Designs
and Patents Act 1988.

10 9 8 7 6 5 4 3 2 1

ISBN 0 340 52462 6

Typeset by Hewer Text Composition Services, Edinburgh
Printed and bound in Great Britain by Cox & Wyman

Hodder and Stoughton Ltd
A Division of Hodder Headline PLC
338 Euston Road
London NW1 3BH

THE CASE AGAINST CHRIST

Also by John Young

Know Your Faith
Our God is Still Too Small
Jesus: The Verdict
Discipleship
Creating Confidence in Evangelism*
Practical Ideas in Evamgelism*
Journeys Into Faith*
Live Your Faith*
80 Practical Suggestions for Evangelism

Indicates the inclusion of material for group discussion

Contents

Foreword
by Lord Blanch

I wish this book had been in my hands when I was a parish priest, because it answers questions my parishioners were asking – or would like to have asked. I wish it had been in my hands when I was a theological college principal, because the author handles important questions at a level those questions deserve. It would have been a good handbook for ordinands about to embark on their first curacy. For that matter I would have been glad to have had it when I was Archbishop of York; I could have saved myself a lot of long letters to irate critics of the Church and puzzled enquirers in search of faith. Altogether it is a remarkable achievement to have combined a lively, entertaining style with genuine scholarship, and a robust personal faith with openness to the objections and criticisms which may be urged against Christianity.

The author is chaplain and teacher in an academic establishment but, as he says, he does not live in an ivory tower. As one-time Chairman of the College I can vouch for his daily involvement in every aspect of college life, amongst the students and the staff. This book is the product of a lively intelligence, honest scholarship and personal commitment to Christ. The reader will learn a lot from this book about the Bible, about religion and science, about suffering and death, and about Christ and the resurrection – and he will learn, too, something about the author, a teacher, a thinker, a humble believer, a man mercifully endowed with a rare sense of humour. He has written the kind of book I would have expected him to write, and I whole-heartedly commend it to you. He has made out a good case for Christ.

Stuart Blanch
March 1986

What the Reviewers said about the First Edition

"This is a fantastic little paperback."

Buzz

"A *must* for anyone who wants to get 'the gen' on popular objections to the Christian faith."

Crusader

"The writing is clear and concise, based on a considerable amount of scholarship, and the text is illustrated by some useful diagrams ... a book to be recommended both to believers and non-believers."

Canon Paul Welsby, Chaplain to the Queen

"The uses of the book will be many – a general reference book ... House groups ... a Lent course."

The Reader

"Well worth getting and passing on."

Bishop Leslie Brown

"If there is a better book at answering popular objections to the Christian Faith, I'd like to see it."

Reconciliation Quarterly

"It really is superb."

Rev. Peter Bye

"A source of delight to me . . . I am going to make a second and third reading and so on."

A Doctor quoted by the Editor of *Challenge*

"The Devil has had a field day with the prejudiced assumption that you have to be some sort of moron to swallow Christianity. This little book does much to set the record straight and to demonstrate that, far from being in conflict, Christian faith goes hand in hand with reason, common sense, and historical fact."

Cliff Richard

"If ministers will put this book to use among all the members of their congregations, the result will be many less defensive Christians, better able to cope with the usual charges against their position."

Church of England Newspaper

"I think it's quite first class."

Bishop Hugh Montefiore

"A terrific little book."

Rev. Margaret Cundiff

"Scholarly . . . very readable."

Evangelism Today

"An incredible achievement . . . a gem."

Rev. Melvin Tinker

"The first edition was excellent and this is even better."

Bishop John B. Taylor

Thank You

Despite its modest size, a large number of people have assisted in the preparation of this book, and I gladly acknowledge their help.

For the typing of numerous drafts I am extremely grateful to Joyce Smith, and to Janet Vere and her marvellous team in the College Secretariat. For efficiency and sound advice, my thanks are due to Carolyn Armitage, the Editor. Stuart Blanch, Archbishop of York until 1983, kindly agreed to write a Foreword, and John Collins' fertile imagination has produced a series of lively drawings. I am indebted to them both – as I am to Rosie Congdon and Naomi Whitehead for checking the typescript, and to Patrick Duncan, Louise Redshaw and Harold Stutely for reading the proofs.

For perceptive comments and lively discussion of the various drafts I am tremendously grateful to Les Bingham, Peter Doble, David Gamble and Louise Redshaw. To protect their good names I should add that I didn't always take their advice. The book's limitations are mine, not theirs.

Above all I am indebted to Jackie Silins, my colleague in the Chaplaincy team, who helped in numerous ways, and to Stuart Coates, a post-graduate student at the College of Ripon and York St. John. Stuart has sifted, researched and double-checked a great deal of material. My confidence in the accuracy of the many facts contained within this book is due mainly to his initiative, industry and intelligence. In addition to their practical help, the supportive friendship offered by Jackie and Stuart – and many others – as I worked to meet deadlines was a considerable encouragement. My family has cheerfully endured my constant scribbling for several months, and to them I warmly dedicate the outcome.

John Young: York
January 1986

Preface to Third Edition

Any book which has a life of nearly a quarter of a century may need revising from time to time. The first edition was much slimmer (and cost 25p!) and then in 1986 I revised that book considerably, expanding it from 110 to 208 pages. For this third edition I have taken the opportunity of updating some of the material. One major new feature is a section of *Suggestions for Group Discussion*.

Many house groups/discussion groups are on the lookout for discussion material, as the reception of *Know Your Faith* (a companion to this book) made clear. *The Case Against Christ* is still intended for individual readers, of course, but I hope that they, too, will spend some time on the suggestions for discussion – partly because the section includes some fine quotations; partly because debating within our own heads can be a fruitful exercise!

I am glad of this opportunity to express my warm gratitude to Bryony Benier, David Mullins, Linda Norman, Kay Taylor and Sharon Winfield for their helpful suggestions and encouragement. I am particularly grateful to John Polkinghorne, who gave generously of his time and unsurpassed knowledge of the interface between Science and Christian Faith. Needless to say, I alone am responsible for the book's imperfections – I fully and freely exonerate my advisers! Above all I wish to express my gratitude to Barbara Thompson, not only for her superb secretarial skills but for her patience and friendship.

John Young: York
March 1994

1

Please Start Here

I often skip the first few pages of books – those sections with boring titles like Preface and Introduction. It is a foolish policy, because authors often give important clues to the way we should approach the book on our lap or at our bedside. So I hope you will read these first few pages – and the other pages too, of course!

About the author

The book will be more personal if I tell you a little about myself. And to further this aim I have asked John Collins to provide a portrait – very brave of me, for he is a cartoonist.

As you read, it will become obvious that I enjoy books. But I enjoy talking and listening even more, and many of the ideas in this book have come from numerous conversations.

For some years I worked in a college, and colleges are often defined as ivory towers – places where the pace of life is slow, and where all conversations are intensely intellectual. Such places may exist, but my college was not one of them!

Now, as then, my work brings me into contact with many young people, and with large numbers of middle-aged and elderly people from all walks of life. Some share my faith; many don't. Our conversations are about the weather, about football, about politics, about families and friends. But quite often I discuss the Christian Faith with believer, agnostic and atheist. Whatever else I should like to claim for this book, I am sure of my ground when I claim this. The chapters which follow are based in the real world. The questions discussed are real questions asked by real people. The objections raised are real objections.

About the contents of this book

First, it is incomplete. There are many objections and problems which I have not attempted to tackle. It has been difficult to decide what to include and what to leave out. Several pages of typing have ended in the wastepaper basket – very painful for an author! But I had to draw the line somewhere, for this is intended to be an inexpensive paperback – not a definitive statement on every issue under the sun.

Second, this book is based on an earlier book with the same title. Some chapters are fairly similar in all editions. But I have reworked the whole book, and added new material. The first edition had twelve chapters and few jokes. This book has twenty-two chapters (some of them very short), six pages of attempted jokes and a guide for group discussion. So – whether or not you have a copy of an earlier edition – I hope you will read this new book, pass it to a friend, and persuade a church leader to use it for discussion groups. But I readily admit to extreme bias in this matter.

Third, the book has a pattern. In particular, an argument is developed from section to section in the second half of the book. However, each chapter is self-contained and some subjects are more difficult than others. So I don't mind in the least if you pick out the chapters which interest you most – although I hope that you will read the entire book eventually.

About the title

I once listened to a discussion entitled "Why I Remain a Christian". It was a good title, demanding thoughtful responses from a group of intelligent, sensitive people.

They had read a fair bit of history, and they knew about the atrocities of the Crusades, and the tortures of the Inquisition. They knew, too, that many powerful minds have argued against the Christian Faith. And they had long experience of church membership – they knew from personal experience about the pettiness, blindness and prejudice which sometimes spoils church life.

Yet they continued to believe. Despite all the problems, their faith in God as Love, and Jesus Christ as Lord, remained unshaken.

Shortly after that, I spent a discussion weekend with a group of students. We invited John Polkinghorne to lead us. He is a Fellow of the Royal Society, and from 1968 to 1979 he was Professor of Mathematical Physics at Cambridge University. Then, in his forties, John believed that God was calling him to full-time ministry within the Church. At the same time, his wife Ruth – also a mathematician – started to train as a nurse.

Since 1989, John has been President of Queens' College, Cambridge. He finds that his scientific understanding *strengthens* his faith in God. He has set out his own position in a fascinating book entitled *The Way The World Is* (Triangle, 1992). He does not have a split personality – half scientist, half Christian. Despite his change of career, he has not turned his back on science. It is John's conviction that God is concerned with *every* aspect of life – not just with religion.

What is it that keeps such people within the Christian Church? This book is an attempt to answer that question. It is written in the knowledge that many important objections continue to be raised against the Christian Faith. It is written in the conviction that – despite these objections – Christianity is true. It is an attempt to act as counsel for the defence in "The Case Against Christ".

About you, the reader

I hope that atheists and agnostics will read this book – especially those who have always assumed that Christianity is a fairy-tale. The fact that several clever, well-balanced people are active Christians – people like those I have just described – does not prove that Christianity is true. But it does suggest *that it is worth investigating*. That is all I ask.

Most people who read this book won't be convinced atheists. It is much more likely that they will be "half-way to faith" – interested in, but unconvinced about, Christianity. More than anyone else, it is for them that I am writing, for I once stood where they stand, and I understand their problems "from the inside".

If this revised and expanded edition of *The Case Against Christ* fares like earlier editions, it will also be read by many Christians who are sensitive to three facts. Firstly, that attacks are often made on their faith by people who hold different views. Secondly, that they sometimes lack the information needed to cope with such attacks. Thirdly, that Christianity is often regarded with a good-natured indifference – which can be harder to cope with than outright criticism.

Objections to Christianity are not new, of course. One of the earliest problems for Christians was the accusation that they were cannibals, because they spoke of "feeding on Christ" in Holy Communion! Centuries later (in 1736), Bishop Butler complained that "many persons" assume that the Christian Faith is fictitious – suitable only for "mirth and ridicule".

It is necessary to think through the different challenges presented in every generation, and I hope that this book might encourage my fellow Christians to do this.

To this end, I shall discuss many questions, debate many issues, and develop many arguments. But throughout I have been haunted by one short sentence – spoken, I think, by Martin Buber, a great Jewish teacher of our century. Concerning belief in God, he asserted, "there are no *evidences*; there are only *witnesses*."

Strictly speaking, this is not true. Certainly there are no knock-down, totally watertight arguments which prove the existence of God. But there are sound reasons for belief, based on accurate, detailed information.

However, most of these reasons come to us in human shape. It is *people* who befriend us, teach us, love us, convince us, nurture us. It is our fellow human beings who share their beliefs, convictions and experiences with us, and point us to their source of strength and inspiration.

I have been greatly privileged to meet, and to read books by, many such witnesses – impressive men, women and young people who ring true. In what follows, I shall draw on them frequently. In one sense this is a book about them, as much as it is about the truths of which they have convinced me.

POSTSCRIPT ON MAKING SENSE OF LIFE

What is life all about? Is it about anything at all? Or are we dumped here without reason or purpose? Do we simply live for seventy or eighty years only to fall off the edge into extinction? Or is there more to it than that?

Most of the time we are too busy to spend long on these deep questions, but from time to time something happens to make us think hard. A friend dies, or someone close to us falls ill, or something wonderful happens, and we find ourselves wondering.

Questions press in on us. Questions like: Can we *really* find God and meaning, truth and love, at the centre of our universe? Or do we live in a cold, uncaring world, which grinds relentlessly on – reducing us all to rubble and dust in the end? The Christian faith does not have glib answers to life's deep questions, but it does claim to have light to shed upon them.

No, our world did *not* "happen" by courtesy of mindless chance; it was loved into existence. No, we do *not* live in a cold, uncaring universe. Yes, we *can* find God and meaning, truth and love, at the centre of our world. That is the Christian gospel – the good news. The even better news is that this is not wishful thinking. This gospel is rooted in history, focused in Jesus and verified in the experience of countless people in every generation, and from every culture and personality type.

The best news of all is that these great qualities: meaning, truth and love – and God himself – can be found, not only at the centre of our universe, but at the heart and centre of our personal, individual lives. And they last throughout eternity.

These are the convictions which under-lie this book and which will be set out for examination.

CONCLUDING QUOTATION

Christianity is a statement which, if false, is of *no* importance, and, if true, of infinite importance. The one thing it cannot be is moderately important – *C. S. Lewis.*

Part I

Questions:
mainly about the Church

Organised Christianity has probably done more to retard the ideals that were its founders than any other agency in the world.

Richard le Gallienne

He cannot have God for his father who has not the Church for his mother.

St. Cyprian

We have been dosing our people with religion, when what they want is not this but the living God.

Frederick Denison Maurice

2

In Brief

Many of the objections we shall examine will require at least one complete chapter, but we shall start by looking at six problems which can be considered rather more briefly.

1. It doesn't matter what you believe, as long as you are sincere

"It doesn't matter what you believe provided you live a good life. Sincerity counts more than anything else. It is what you *do* that matters, not what you believe."

Statements like this are common when people discuss religion. The trouble is that they oversimplify, for beliefs and actions are tied up together.

If you believe that the gods are pleased by human sacrifice, then it is tough on your children. If your witch doctor believes that a hole bored in your head will cure headaches, it is tough on you. If the terrorist who hijacks your plane sincerely believes in his cause, you are in for a rough time.

We are right to value sincerity, but false beliefs – even sincerely held false beliefs – can be disastrous. Indeed, the more sincere your "doctor" is about boring a hole in your head, the worse it will be. And the most sincere terrorist is the most dangerous of all.

Belief governs action.

Why was it that the Nazis caused such havoc in Europe? It was because they *believed* that the German people were a super-race, with a destiny to rule the world. Why did the American government cause such suffering by dropping an atomic bomb on Hiroshima on 6th August, 1945? It was because they *believed* that this would shorten the war (or that it would "impress" the Russians, depending on your view of history).

This connection between faith and action applies to everything. It is what a person *believes* that makes him or her an atheist, or a Buddhist, or a Christian, or a Communist – or a terrorist. We organise society on the basis of beliefs and convictions.

The most brilliant scientist cannot get a government post until he has been security checked. They want to know what he *believes*. Until they know this, he is regarded as a risk. It is because of the strong link between belief and behaviour that some regimes go in for brainwashing.

Our beliefs are vitally important.

2. Religion is dull

If someone at a wedding drinks lemonade, believing it to be champagne, she may think that champagne is dull. But she will be wrong, for she is passing judgment on the wrong thing.

Most people have had some experience of "religion". And they have found it boring. Lack of enthusiasm in the singing, lack of warmth in the welcome, appeals for funds – things like this have put them off. On the other hand, fewer people have experienced living, vital, Christianity over a period of time. But because of their experience of religion, many people dismiss Christianity, for they think these are the same thing.

It is rather like a vaccination. You can be prevented from

catching the real thing, by a smaller dose of something similar.

The actor Paul Jones played a leading role in *Guys and Dolls* in London's West End. He was put off religion at school. Some school religion is good, but in his case the stress was entirely on *duty*. There was no joy. He found it boring and unrelated to his life. Many years later he came to a living faith in Christ, and experienced a new quality of life. He began to understand the words of Jesus: "I have come that they may have life, and have it to the full" (John 10:10).

Religion can be deadly dull. It is Christ who brings it to life. *He* can transform religion into vital, adventurous faith. When he does so, the outward expressions of that faith – worship, prayer, Bible reading, fellowship – come to life as well.

There is all the difference in the world between formal religion and real Christianity. Mind you, we are forbidden by Jesus to attempt to decide whose religion is formal, and whose is really alive. To start judging other people in this way is a very slippery slope indeed. *We* can't tell; only God can.

Closely related to this objection is the view that Christianity is irrelevant. The central Christian claim tackles this head-on. We believe that Jesus Christ is alive and active in our world. If we will allow him to do so, he will guide us, inspire us, strengthen and transform us.

This is not just theory. I think of a rather lonely young man who was drifting aimlessly, whose life is now full of purpose and friends. I think of a vicious criminal who left prison and worked hard to support other people in need.

Why the change? Each of them speaks of the power of Christ in his life. In this book I shall introduce you to many people whose lives have been deeply influenced in the same way, and for the same reason. You must decide for yourself whether or not they are deluded.

3. A bad case of wishful thinking

At Christmas, many churches are crowded. People flock in to sing the familiar carols; to see the candlelit churches; to watch the children's Nativity plays. It's all very magical – and I love it!

For some people, Christmas means a large dose of wistful, wishful thinking. If only . . . if only it could be true. But all that talk about heavenly choirs and guiding stars takes a bit of believing. And it isn't too difficult to think of an alternative explanation for the too-early pregnancy of an attractive young woman.

So let's brighten up our lives for an hour or two. Let's pretend – but not for too long. Boxing Day will soon be here – and endless turkey soup to remind us that Christmas is just an interlude.

Wishful thinking is a real danger. We want something to be true, so we convince ourselves that it *is* true. Perhaps Christians are those who never get back to reality. Perhaps Christianity is a case of pretending that Boxing Day will never come.

Perhaps . . . but the trouble with that line of reasoning is that it works in two directions.

Aldous Huxley, author of *Brave New World* and many other books, admitted that for many years he asserted his atheism for just this reason. The idea of God was extremely *in*convenient. He didn't want the world to have any long-term meaning, because he wanted to live without irksome moral controls. So he chose to believe that God does not exist, and that the world has no meaning. Later in life, he was honest enough to admit his motives for believing this.

No doubt there are Christians who desperately want the Christian Faith to be true – perhaps because they are afraid of death, or for some other reason. But as we have seen, there are non-Christians who would greatly prefer that it wasn't true. And many Christians often wish that the way of Christ wasn't so demanding.

The assertion that "it's all wishful thinking" can work *for* and *against* Christianity. It leaves untouched the really central question: yes, but is it *true* or *false*?

This is an appropriate point to say a word about the famous "placebo effect" (you take aspirin and your headache disappears. I take what *I think* is aspirin, and my headache disappears). This is sometimes applied to religion by its critics who say: Christianity works for you because *you believe it to be true*, not because it *is* true.

Perhaps. Perhaps not. Certainly the placebo effect is a reality – in medicine at least. In trials, more than one-third of those who were given what they thought was morphine (but wasn't) reported a reduction in pain. But this leaves about 60 per cent for whom belief without substance *didn't* work.

I would estimate that the same kind of figure might apply to a religion without any basis in fact and reality. The placebo effect seems to be clearest in neurotic subjects. Again, while some Christians are mentally unstable, many others are very well balanced indeed.

4. You don't need to go to church to be a Christian

If this statement means that you can be a nice person without going to church, then it is obviously true. But if it means that you can be a follower of Jesus Christ without joining a church, the assertion is rather more problematic.

For one thing, the word disciple means "learner". If we really do want to learn about the way of Jesus, then church isn't a bad place to start. But there is another reason too. Jesus chose twelve disciples and he taught them as a group. From that moment on, his followers had to learn to get on with each other – and it wasn't always easy.

He made it clear that they must work *together*. Like it or not, they were to think of themselves as a community and as a family. In some families, various members don't meet together, nor speak to one another. When this happens, we know that things have gone wrong. The same is true of the Church – the family of God.

Behind this common objection, there is another assumption too – the assumption that worship isn't very important. I would want to argue with that as well. At first sight it doesn't seem to have much to do with the real world – but first impressions can be wrong. Worship isn't a hobby for those who like singing hymns; it is more serious than that.

In worship we are *admitting* something important about ourselves – that we are dependent upon one another and upon God, and that we need his forgiveness and grace. Even more important, in worship we are *doing* something about the state of the world – at least, that is the Christian claim.

Archbishop Michael Ramsey told a pointed parable. It concerns a man with boils, who visited his doctor. The doctor told his patient that he couldn't treat the boils, without treating the poison in his body. The same is true of the human race. We have several nasty boils in the social and moral order: the build-up of weapons; antagonism between different races; the great gap between rich and poor; growing environmental problems . . .

To deal with them properly, we need to go to the root, and to deal with the poison in the system. Michael Ramsey concludes that worship helps us to deal with that poison: "The root is the right relation of man to Creator: and when Christians are concerned about what they call worship they are concerned, not with something remote or escapist, but with the root of the world's predicament."

5. God was an astronaut!

We live in a scientific age, but belief in powers and forces which science cannot explain remains strong. Astrology is amazingly popular, and horoscopes abound. For many people this is "just a bit of fun". Others – some of them highly educated – take it very seriously indeed.

Astrology is only one aspect. On holiday I visited a small library in Sussex. The "Religious Books" section was light on serious theology, but heavy on sensation, and on such subjects as spiritualism and ESP (extra-sensory perception – telepathy, etc.). Three large books probed the question: was God an astronaut? The date-stamp pages indicated high popularity.

It is clear that we modern people have not "come of age" after all. We mix our scientific view of the world with a large dose of superstition and credulity.

I thought hard about tackling some of these issues in this book, but it became clear that *general* arguments would not do. Each piece of evidence (or "evidence") needs to be examined carefully, and that would take too much space. So, with some reluctance, I have left these problems on one side. But I will make two observations.

First, a word to those who are interested in the "was God an astronaut?" question. This has been popularised by Erich von Daniken in a whole series of books. These have sold in vast numbers and I salute him as a fine – and highly imaginative! – communicator. But I don't know of a single expert in the fields which he covers who lends any support to his views.

If this subject interests you, I suggest you read *Some Trust in Chariots* edited by E. W. Castle and B. B. Thiering. The book contains chapters by sixteen experts whose personal beliefs range from Christian to agnostic. Between them they cover a variety of specialisms from ancient history to modern engineering. The engineer examines in detail some of von Daniken's claims and speaks for the other contributors when he says: "It seems fatuous of Herr von Daniken to have built such an extensive theory on such readily disprovable premises. He should have done his homework better!" Sadly, Castle's book is out of print, but it is available from libraries.

Second, we must not lump all these fringe subjects together. For example, ESP is an important area of study, requiring careful research. As for astrology – the most popular of all – I will risk unpopularity by advising people who dabble in this to leave it alone. The Christian Faith does not encourage us to peer into the future. Instead, it encourages us to face the future with trust and confidence in the living God. People who have future events in their lives "revealed" to them by horoscopes or fortune-tellers often tend (perhaps unconsciously) to let this information shape their lives.

6. Christianity is humourless

At first sight – and perhaps at second sight, too – this appears to be the case. Exuberance and joy have an obvious place in a faith which celebrates resurrection and life. But worship varies in mood. As we keep watch with Jesus in Gethsemane we are quiet and still. As we consider Calvary we are solemn and serious. Perhaps we shall be moved to tears.

The same is true of the Bible. Jesus encourages those who

mourn, "for they will be comforted". St. James bids us to "grieve, mourn and wail". Tears are not out of place as we consider the spiritual poverty of our lives, the bitter divisions in our world, and the cost of our redemption.

This is not the whole story though. Overall, the New Testament is a happy book. Read it, and a range of positive words stand out: joy, rejoice, blessed (which means happy). And there are jokes in the New Testament. Some of these are puns which don't translate well from the Greek. Some of them have been blunted by familiarity.

I am quite sure that Jesus' teaching would often have raised a smile – and probably a guffaw or two. A camel trying to get through the eye of a needle, or a man with a plank in his eye (as opposed to a speck of sawdust) would not be out of place on the Goon Show or in a Lenny Henry sketch.

So if I need weighty justification for including a few jokes in this book, that would be it. But perhaps I need no deeper excuse than to say that I enjoy jokes, and that you, dear reader (as a Victorian author might say), may well need a break from serious reading from time to time. If you find that a chapter gets tough, or if your eyes begin to close, turn to a page entitled *Take a Break*!

*   *   *

We have looked at some of the objections which are raised against Christianity, and we shall be considering several more. This may give the impression of a defensive "back to the wall" attitude.

In fact, of course, Christians are not alone in facing problems raised by their beliefs. For example, a group of agnostics published a book entitled *Objections to Humanism*, in which they spoke of the difficulties which *they* face as a result of *their* beliefs.

Every view of life raises problems, and it is important that they should be faced and discussed, not ignored or buried.

TAKE A BREAK (1)
A LITTLE CHILD SHALL LEAD THEM

When church services are too long

The church service was far too long for Billy aged seven. He looked around for interesting distractions. "What's that?" he asked, pointing to the names on the roll of honour, affixed to the wall. "Those are the people who died in the Services," whispered his mother. "Oh," said Billy, intrigued, "did they die in the morning services or the evening services?"

* * *

When the truth is too hard to bear

A primary school youngster was asked to write about the summer holidays. She showed her composition to Mum. "Our Mary didn't go to Africa!" protested Mum. "She went to Gloucester." "I know," said Jane, "but I couldn't spell Gloucester."

* * *

A shepherd to his flock

A young boy sat near the front at the Confirmation Service. He was intrigued by the shepherd's crook which the bishop carried. At Sunday School the following week he was asked to write about the Confirmation. He wrote: "Last Sunday I sat near the bishop. Now I know what a crook looks like."

* * *

A true story

We attended a modern pantomime based on the Nativity story. King Herod stormed about the stage, looking for little boys and ranting "Fe, fi, fo, fum. I smell the blood of an Englishman." Suddenly he stopped. "Ah, ha," he shouted. "I smell a little boy." There was a pause. Then a little voice from the front row called out indignantly, "Well, it wasn't me!"

* * *

Rewriting history

They were casting the school Nativity Play. Michael badly wanted to play one of the central figures. But he and his teacher didn't always get on too well, so he was given a safe minor part as the innkeeper. "I'll learn her," muttered Michael to himself. After many hitchless rehearsals, the big day came. The hall was packed with parents, teachers and governors. Along came the Holy Family. "Is there any room in the inn?" asked Joseph. Michael grinned and threw open the doors. "Plenty of room," he replied. "Come on in."

POSTSCRIPT ON BRAINWASHING

Some religious sects brainwash people into their ways and beliefs. Aware of this danger, when I taught Religious Education, I was concerned to *educate*, not *indoctrinate*, my pupils. I wanted them to think for themselves, not simply to accept my views second hand.

In my clearer moments, I realised how absurd I was to worry about indoctrinating those children in an hour per week – for many of them were thoroughly brainwashed already!

Some were indoctrinated by the ad-man; they believed that happiness came from piling up possessions. Others were brainwashed into believing that religion is irrelevant to life. They didn't *think* about these things: they simply took them for granted.

The same is true of many adults, too. In inviting unbelievers to read this book, I am being cheeky. For I am asking them to acknowledge that their present views about Christianity may result, not from hard, well-informed thought – but from prejudice, or from inadequate information, or from a second-hand acceptance of other people's opinions and attitudes.

I hope that they will forgive my boldness, which arises from my own experience. For that was my position with regard to the Christian Faith for many years – and I sadly confess that it remains my position in some areas of life, even now.

3

Those Hypocritical Christians!

In York – the city in which I live – there is a famous medieval street called the Shambles. Old buildings lean across a narrow cobbled road. If you lean out of one upstairs window, you can touch the house opposite. It is very picturesque, and a "must" for tourists.

One house in the street was the home of Margaret Clitherow – a devout Roman Catholic who lived in the sixteenth century. Accused of harbouring priests, she refused to plead her case – in order to save her children from being forced to witness against her.

As a result she was crushed to death by heavy weights, on the orders of a "Christian" state. That terrible incident reminds us that anyone who tries to defend the record of the Christian Church has a tough job.

Christian history is very mixed. There have been plenty of saints; there has been a great deal of courage; there has been a lot of love. But only a fool would pretend that this tells the whole story. Christian history is blackened by the execution of innocent people simply because they were Protestant or Catholic; by the enforced "conversion" of whole populations; by the unwillingness of many in the Church to fight against social evils. And I frequently talk with people who say that they don't attend church because they don't like the people who do! Words like "unfriendly", "clique" and "hypocrite" often come into such conversations.

Jesus was once asked to state the greatest commandment. In reply, he summarised the Old Testament Law: Love God with all your strength, and love your neighbour as yourself. This is crystal clear. Why then has the Church so often strayed so far from his teaching? I will offer three reasons.

1. Non-Christian leaders in the Church

When the Church became very powerful, it was invaded by ambition. Men with little regard for the teaching of Christ, and far from the Spirit of Christ, held high positions within the Church of Christ. Their concern was not to follow Jesus of Nazareth, but to gain power, prestige or wealth.

Perhaps this was inevitable during those centuries when everyone in Europe who was not a Jew or a Muslim was automatically regarded as a Christian. Which brings us to the second reason:

2. Elastic use of the word Christian

Over the years, the word "Christian" has been stretched in two directions. *On the one hand* it is often used as a compliment. I remember hearing someone describe his friend as a Communist and an atheist. He added, "but he's as good a Christian as you or me." He wanted to say that he thought his friend was a good man, so he used the word "Christian".

If he was using the word correctly, then it would be intolerable for anyone to say "I am a Christian." That would be the worst kind of boasting. But the follower of Christ does not mean "I am a specially good person" when he claims to be a Christian.

It is easy to see how the word came to be used in this way. Followers of Jesus are expected to lead good lives. But to apply this word to all people whom we admire, whether or not they follow Jesus Christ, simply causes confusion. After all, his name makes up two-thirds of the word. Besides, it is unfair to a large number of atheists and agnostics to saddle them with a word they don't want.

The word "Christian" began its life in the New Testament, and it is used there, not as a compliment, but as a *description*. It describes a person who believes that Jesus Christ is the Son of God, and who – often unsuccessfully – tries to follow and worship him.

This is the way in which the word is used throughout this book. When I call a person a non-Christian, I am not intending to insult him or her. Nor am I suggesting that he or she is inferior to the person who is a Christian. The phrase is used simply to record the fact that this person does not acknowledge Jesus Christ as Lord and Saviour.

On the other hand, the word "Christian" has been watered down. Far from being used as a compliment, or referring to an individual committed to the way of Christ, it is often applied to almost anyone who was born in a "Christian country". "Christian" has become a convenient label, helping us to distinguish one cultural group from another, such as Muslims or Jews.

A wry story from Northern Ireland tells of a young man who was asked whether he was Catholic or Protestant. "I'm not a Christian," he replied. "I'm an agnostic. But I'm a Protestant agnostic"! This illustrates all too clearly the muddle over words produced by twenty centuries of Christian history.

3. Christians are sinners

Convenient as it would be, we can't blame *all* the bad things in the Church onto people who aren't really Christian at all. Christians are sinners, and they share much of the prejudice and ignorance of the age in which they live. No doubt many soldiers in the Crusades were devout men who sincerely believed in their cause. From our viewpoint, they were sincerely wrong.

So the objection remains. Christians are *not* good people.

However, there is one saving factor. They *know* they are not, and it is for this very reason that they find Jesus Christ so important.

Jesus is not just a great teacher, or a fine example. In the Bible he is called a *Saviour*. The word means "Saver" or "Rescuer". He rescues people from their selfishness, their indifference to the needs of others, their pride, their jealousy, their snobbishness, their lust – those things which spoil our lives, and which sometimes make us ashamed.

Jesus spoke of himself as a doctor. "It is not the healthy who need a doctor, but the sick," he said. "I have not come to call the righteous, but sinners" (Mark 2:17). Christians are sinners who have responded to this invitation.

When Christians go to church, they are not trying to impress other people with their uprightness and goodness. This would be like going to hospital to show how healthy you are!

One of the most important aspects of any church service is the confession of our sins. We publicly acknowledge our moral and spiritual poverty – and we ask for God's forgiveness and strength. Each church is like an outpatients' department in a hospital for the spiritually and morally sick.

In some ways the marvel is, not that the Church fails so often, but that it has done any good at all. For it is made up of self-confessed moral failures.

Christians are not basically good, respectable people. They are thoroughly dissatisfied people. They are dissatisfied with *themselves*. They know that they are selfish; or that they cannot control their tempers; or that they are jealous; or greedy; or lazy; or . . . It is because they know their own shortcomings, and their own great needs, that they have gone to the one Person who can help them: Jesus Christ, the Great Physician.

But sometimes a cure takes a long time. Especially when someone has a really bad dose of an illness. Sometimes the protest that "Christians are no better than anyone else" is not true, because it does not go far enough. Some Christians are a lot *worse*, by ordinary standards.

For example, there are criminals, drug addicts, and alcoholics who are real Christians. Their lives are not always changed in an instant. But because a cure ultimately depends on the power of Christ, and not on the individual Christian, a successful outcome is certain in the long run.

The disease of sin, no matter how severe, will always be healed eventually, if the person puts himself into Christ's hands. The trouble is, that we all have something wrong with us, and an apparently mild attack will get steadily worse, if it is not treated.

POSTSCRIPT ON SIN AND GUILT

This book has hardly begun, and already we are deep into talk about sin. Sure confirmation that the Church is too concerned with sin and guilt!

In fact, you won't find much more about these particular subjects in this book, but it is worth spending a few paragraphs looking at this particular objection. Perhaps it was best summed up by the parishioner who complained: "Until our new vicar arrived, we didn't know what sin was"!

First, a word about guilt. This has had a bad press from some psychologists, and it is often assumed that guilt feelings are always bad. Of course, vague, unfocused feelings of guilt are unhealthy. But a sense of guilt isn't always a bad thing. If I steal your wallet, your wife, or your reputation, I am guilty, and there is only hope for me – and for you – if I *feel guilty*. A psychopath would feel no guilt; a healthy person would feel lots. But guilt needs to be put to work. If it doesn't lead to repentance and restoration, it is useless.

Second, let's turn our attention to sin. The most important point to notice is that Christianity isn't in the least interested in sin. It is intensely interested in the *forgiveness* of sins, and *liberation* from sin's power – which is a different matter altogether.

Sin can be defined in various ways. One of the best definitions was written on a wall of the Cathedral of Notre Dame in Paris: "Sin is a refusal to grow bigger". We sin when we refuse to enlarge our vision and concerns. We sin when we settle for an undemanding life, and refuse to accept the challenge of discipleship.

Perhaps the simplest definition of sin is "breaking God's law". Looked at like this, most people are against sin. Read the Ten Commandments (Exod. 20) and you will probably agree with most of them. For most of us are against being killed, or having our property stolen, or our reputation damaged.

Another way of defining sin is as self-centredness. Most of us are against this too – in other people at least. Think of a totally selfish character in a TV soap opera – someone whose whole life is centred on him/herself and whose ambitions take no account of other people's feelings.

Christianity is against that approach to life, because it is intensely damaging – to the person who lives like that, and to the people with whom he or she lives and works. In the end, lives that are lived in that way become sad and empty. In saying that the Church is against this approach to life, we are saying that Christ is *for* their opposites. He stands for thoughtfulness, kindness, forgiveness, co-operation, openness, and generosity.

To some extent, all of us are like the selfish character in the TV series. We all settle too easily for a comfortable life, and we don't fight, give, or pray hard enough for other people's rights and happiness. So we mustn't point the finger too readily – except at ourselves, perhaps. We *all* need to be challenged, inspired and strengthened if we are to get a wider vision, and a bigger heart.

Which is where Jesus comes in. He came to deal with sin and to remove guilt. To put this another way: he wants to free us from fear, anxiety and self-centredness, so that we can live in joy, peace and love.

This was summed up powerfully by Harry Williams, an Anglican monk who was Prince Charles's tutor at Cambridge: "Being a Christian means . . . being people in whom his (Jesus') life and character and power are manifest and energised . . . Christian experience is not so much a matter of imitating a leader . . . as accepting and receiving a new quality of life – a life infinitely more profound and dynamic and meaningful than human life without Christ."

CONCLUDING QUOTATION

A real Christian is not only a good and well-intentioned person but a man or woman for whom Jesus Christ is ultimately decisive; for whom Jesus – not Caesar, not another god, not money, sex, power, or pleasure – is Lord – *Hans Küng*.

4

The Credit Side

If we think about the Inquisition, and about the violent quarrels between some Roman Catholics and Protestants in Northern Ireland, we shall – alas – be thinking about facts. If we concentrate on the dullness of some church services and the refusal of many church-goers to "get involved" we shall, sadly, be thinking about more facts. But not *all* the facts.

If Jesus Christ really *does* help his followers to overcome their selfishness, and if he really *does* pour his love into their lives, we should expect to find some practical evidence of this. We are not disappointed. There *is* a credit side. The failures are great, but the successes are tremendous too.

Christianity certainly has no monopoly on love, goodness and social action. But enough men and women have done great things *because* of their Christian faith, to show that the accusation that Christians are unfriendly, uninvolved, or hypocritical, is not always true. Here are a few examples, taken from the early days of the Church, from the Victorian Church, and from our own times.

1. The Early Church

The early Christians were impressive. In one sense they were very ordinary, and they failed a great deal. The fact remains that they "conquered" the brutal, well-organised, Roman Empire. They captured it for Jesus Christ and for his gospel of love, with a single weapon – the quality of their lives. They showed love in a world which valued indifference. They demonstrated joy and deep happiness in a world where people settled for pleasure. They practised forgiveness in a world which believed in harsh revenge.

Early in the fourth century, the Christian Faith had become the official religion of the Roman Empire – with very mixed blessings for that Faith. Later in that same century the anti-Christian Emperor Julian came to the throne. He accused the Christians of atheism because they believed in one invisible God – and a God who could not be seen or touched was no God at all! He was determined to reinstate the pagan gods. Julian lost his crusade, and he was honest enough to say why. His words are impressive because he was an opponent of the Christian way.

"Atheism (i.e. Christian Faith) has been specially advanced through the loving service rendered to strangers and through their care for the burial of the dead. It is a scandal that there is not a single Jew who is a beggar, and that the godless Galileans care not only for their own poor but for ours as well; while those who belong to us look in vain for the help that we should render them."

The "loving service" of the early Christians challenged and changed deep-seated attitudes. Antony Bridge, a convert from atheism who became Dean of Guildford, preached a powerful sermon in which he asked: why value love at all? He went on to admit that this sounds like an idiotic question, because most of us assume that love is a virtue. Then he made an important contrast:

"But other civilisations have assumed no such thing. Courage, stoic endurance, the search for wisdom, intellectual integrity, strength, detachment – these are the virtues normally worshipped by mankind and preached by his many religions. And love is a contradiction of many of them."

Despite this, most of us continue to believe in love – even if we don't always practise it. We do so because of thousands of years of teaching by Jews and Christians – and because love is emphasised by modern psychologists. That was Antony Bridge's conclusion.

2. Yesterday's Church

The Church of the last century is often criticised. It is too easily assumed that nineteenth-century Christians were universally hypocritical – praying in their churches on Sunday, and exploiting in their factories on Monday. Sadly, there were – and are – hypocrites in the Church, but this view does not express the whole truth.

For one thing, there were many working-class Christians. It is tragically true that the Church lost touch with many workers during the Industrial Revolution. But not with all workers. Indeed, Christianity played a central role in the struggle by British workers to form trades' unions.

In 1830, Dorset farm labourers earned nine shillings a week. By 1834 this had been reduced to seven shillings, with the threat of a further one-shilling reduction. With George Loveless as their leader, and the Vicar of Tolpuddle as an intermediary, the men tried to negotiate with their employers. Promises were made but not kept. Eventually the men formed a union – the Friendly Society of Agricultural Labourers – for which six of them were sentenced to deportation. Five of these "Tolpuddle Martyrs" were Methodists. The Loveless brothers were local preachers. Their ability to organise and to speak in public grew out of their Christian roots.

The famous . . . The involvement of some Victorian Christians in crusades *against* grinding poverty and *for* social reform is legendary. Societies founded then continue to be honoured throughout the world.

Foremost among these are organisations for children: the National Children's Home (a Methodist Foundation), Spurgeon's Homes (a Baptist Foundation), Muller's Homes (Evangelical Brethren), the Children's Society (Anglican). And excellent work is done in the many local authority homes which grew from this Christian soil.

The most famous individual in this field is "Dr." Barnardo with his motto, written in brick: "No destitute child ever refused admission". It was a heroic promise, given the large number of homeless children in London. The motto itself resulted from tragedy. A boy called "Carrots" was given money and told to return later, because the home was full. He did not return, for he died of exposure.

Yet London nearly lost Barnardo to China, for he seriously considered missionary work. The movement which he started has spread to many other countries.

In his book *Civilisation*, Lord Clark – not himself a Christian – wrote about the Quaker Elizabeth Fry, whose "spiritual influence on the prisoners at Newgate was really a miracle". He went on to pay tribute to William Wilberforce and Lord Shaftesbury. For their struggles against slavery, and for a host of social reforms, he described them as two of the greatest names "in the history of humanitarianism".

Each met fierce opposition, each based his life and work on the Bible, and each found support from other Christian leaders. For example, one week before he died, John Wesley – founder of Methodism – wrote to Wilberforce. It was probably his last letter: "Go on in the name of God and in the power of his might, till even American slavery (the vilest that ever saw the sun) shall vanish away before it."

Then there were the Christian Socialists. Men like Charles Kingsley, the Anglican clergyman whose *Water Babies* focused on the plight of chimney boys. Women like Margaret MacMillan whose vision and energy helped to revolutionise education. She insisted that schools should be happy places. She introduced nursery schools, swimming pools, and school meals into Bradford, where rickets was common.

Her ideas fired other imaginations, and her influence continues today. In Parliament in 1944 she was described as "the greatest educationist this country ever produced". J. B. Priestley gave a typically passionate, gritty accolade: "Such persons, single-minded, pure in heart, blazing with selfless love, are the jewels of our species . . . if it were not for them, plus a few glorious artists, this world would be one huge ashpit."

In any list of those "blazing with selfless love" we need to include William Booth, founder of the Salvation Army.

. . . and the less famous: Barnardo, Wilberforce and Elizabeth Fry are well known. But who has heard of R. W. Lowry? On 13th November, 1885, the *Church Times* published a letter in which he asked for support for a home established by "two ladies . . . with the warm approval of the Bishop of the Diocese".

The home was for twelve young girls who had been rescued from child prostitution – a work paralleled in our own century by Father Joe Williamson of Stepney. The women wanted to take in many more children, and to help them, "till the children are able to help themselves". No doubt many others – like R. W. Lowry and the "two ladies" – did their work with little recognition, and with no subsequent fame.

Limitations: The work of these reformers can be criticised. Each of them had limitations and prejudices – especially when judged by twentieth-century eyes. The fact remains that the energy, vision and compassion which sprang from their faith in Christ improved the quality of life for millions.

Their labours were sometimes warmly appreciated. At Shaftesbury's funeral in October 1885, thousands lined the streets – some of the factory workers, miners, chimney boys, ragged children (Shaftesbury knew and helped Barnardo), flower girls, farm workers, "lunatics" and criminals who had benefited from his reforms.

A poignant cry went up: "Our Earl's gone." Shaftesbury Avenue and Piccadilly's "Eros" are his memorials in brick, metal and stone. His greater memorial is thousands of lives touched by his love and energy.

Outside Britain: Britain had no monopoly on compassion. Father Damien, a Belgian priest, volunteered for work among leprosy sufferers who were treated as outcasts. His inspiring work on the Hawaiian island of Molokai involved building houses and providing a water supply, in addition to elementary medical care. He contracted leprosy himself in 1885, and died in 1889, at the age of 49.

Since then enormous progress has been made, much of it pioneered by Christians – both missionaries and nationals. Mary Verghese, Paul Brand and Stanley Browne come to mind. When the latter was awarded the Royal African Society's medal in 1970, the Council spoke of his "unrivalled knowledge of leprosy research and control".

The task is still enormous. Only a small fraction of the millions of leprosy sufferers in the modern world are receiving treatment. But this brings us to the present day, and to our final section in this chapter.

3. Today's Church

A story is told about an English archbishop who visited America. On arrival he held a news conference. *Question*: will you be visiting a night club in New York? *Clever answer*: are there any night clubs in New York? *Headlines in newspaper*: Archbishop's first question – are there any night clubs in New York?

He was putty in their hands. This is one view of the Church strongly pressed on television. Christian leaders are shown as innocents abroad – humble do-gooders, who do no good.

Off the television screen, comments are sometimes harsher. In our college chapel we had a board for prayer requests. Slips of paper were provided which began, *Please pray for* . . . One morning I found the following "request". *Please pray for* . . . "All Christians, that they may become less sanctimonious . . ." Painfully, I realised how we Christians appear to some people who don't share our faith.

But despite its weak television image, and despite its many failures, the Church this century continues to be impressive in many ways. The work of Mother Teresa on behalf of the poor and dying is universally recognised, but she does not stand alone.

Resisting evil: When Hitler came to power in Germany, he tried to use the Church to gain support. To their shame, some church leaders agreed, not seeing the monstrous shape of things to come. But some refused to co-operate. They formed the "Confessing Church" in Germany, and throughout the entire period of Hitler's power, they opposed him. E. H. Robertson, an expert on the Church in Germany during the war period, wrote:

> The resistance of the Confessing Church to the policy of Hitler continued into and through the war years. It alone survived the bitter attack on all opposition and non-conformity, and raised its voice constantly in 2,000 pulpits and in every possible way.

Black Church leaders spearheaded the struggle for civil rights in the USA in the 1960s. This movement was led from the front by Martin Luther King, a Baptist pastor, who – following Gandhi – advocated non-violent resistance. He preached a sermon entitled "A Tough Mind and a Tender Heart". These seven words sum him up.

After his assassination on 4th April, 1968, one black man went into the streets to shoot the first white man he met. Martin Luther King would have regarded this as a total failure for his message. In contrast he would have drawn encouragement from his wife Coretta. As she discussed her husband's murder with their children, she urged them not to hate the assassin.

As I write, a similar struggle dominates South Africa. The outcome is uncertain but the need for forgiveness, reconciliation, hope and new beginnings is clear. How many will be able to walk that path? A great milestone was reached with the signing of a non-racial Constitution on 17th November, 1993. Many Christians – black, coloured and white – have shown fine leadership in that troubled and divided land. Archbishop Desmond Tutu is the best known; there are many others.

Perhaps the fact that Nelson Mandela and F. W. de Klerk share a common faith in Christ enabled them to overcome such immense obstacles.

Many present-day leaders point to the influence upon them of Bishop Trevor Huddleston, and of Chief Albert Luthuli. The latter – a Christian Zulu leader – was awarded the Nobel Peace Prize in 1960. Whether the message of reconciliation embraced by these leaders will win enough hearts and minds to heal the deep divisions which still exist, is impossible to predict. The outcome has enormous implications for us all.

Vision and commitment: Over the past few decades many caring and crusading agencies have sprung up. *Shelter* is one example. This organisation was formed on 1st December, 1966, in order to combat the enormous misery and suffering caused by the problem of homelessness in Britain.

It is not a specifically Christian organisation, but it finds a place here because Christians were prominent among those who set it up. This is clearly seen from the fact that Shelter resulted from the united concern of five organisations: the Notting Hill Housing Trust, the Catholic Housing Aid Society, the National Federation of Housing Associations, Christian Action, and the British Churches Housing Trust.

Of the five individuals singled out for special mention by Shelter in connection with the launching of the movement, three were Christian leaders. Bruce Kenrick, a Christian minister, was Shelter's first Chairman.

Samaritans is another example. Like Shelter, it is not a specifically Christian organisation. Regardless of their beliefs, men and women are invited to become helpers, provided they are willing to give their time, as listeners and befrienders. The phones are answered night and day.

In Britain each year about 5,000 people commit suicide (4,673 in 1992) and some 200,000 make an "unsuccessful" attempt. Many people believe that the Samaritans have played a key role in pegging numbers at this level. One thing is certain: their telephones and offices receive tens of thousands of callers each year.

The oak grew from an acorn. In 1953, a London rector became aware that a large number of people were suicidal and despairing. Chad Varah invited desperate people to ring Mansion House 9000. Within twenty years his simple idea had grown into an international movement.

Another burst of imaginative, creative energy has resulted in the establishment of many hospices in Britain, over the past few decades. It was largely the vision and energy of far-sighted Christians which led to this. The work of the hospice movement in helping people to die with dignity is spreading. Recently, hospices have been founded for children. The first of those – Helen House in Oxford – was established by Anglican nuns in 1982. Sadly, it has been necessary to found yet another Christian hospice – the Mildmay Hospital for AIDS sufferers.

A great deal of good work is done in Christ's name, with little publicity – and little desire for publicity. Work with young people, centres for homeless men and women, communities for drug addicts and drop-outs, teas for elderly people, homes for handicapped people.

Jean Vanier is founder of l'Arche (the Ark) – a network of small communities providing love and care for mentally handicapped people. He summed up the driving force behind many who give their spare time, or devote their lives, to these enterprises: "We all have to choose between two ways of being crazy: the foolishness of the Gospel and the nonsense of the values of our world".*

From many other areas which merit comment, I want to pay tribute to the work for peace of the Quakers and Brethren, and to the work on the "fringes" of society of the Church Army and the Salvation Army. One of the latter's numerous enterprises is a highly professional Missing Persons Bureau. For many years, they have regarded the fact that large numbers of people simply "disappear" as a human problem requiring specialist knowledge. Each year their Bureau helps restore

---

* One reader expressed surprise that a Christian should say that the Gospel is "foolish". If in doubt, look up 1 Corinthians 1:25!

nearly 5,000 people to lost relatives. Always, they observe the highest standards of confidentiality.

The local Church: The national and international organisations listed above make a direct impact upon thousands of people, week by week. It remains true that the Christian Faith is mediated to most people by their local churches. For despite the much-publicised decline in church attendance, the network of local churches continues to attract large numbers. It is still the case that many more people are in churches on Sundays than in football stadiums on Saturdays.

The quality of church life is extremely patchy. The conduct of some clergy is embarrassing – I think of the vicar who scolded his Carol Service congregation for not attending church more often. I could understand their reluctance! And it is all too possible to go to church as a stranger, and to remain unwelcomed by a single member of the congregation.

At the other end of the spectrum are congregations with vision, warmth, energy and commitment. I visit a wide range of churches, large and small. You will gather that I am a not-uncritical observer. But I can record with total honesty the fact that I am often impressed with the imagination, care, support and vitality which I find.

I once came across this small note in a parish magazine: "Saint Luke's exists to serve the people of this parish in whatever way possible in Christ's name. The Vicar is available at all times – should help be needed. Do not hesitate to get in touch with him at any time of day or night."

The man who wrote that is often very stretched. He is chaplain to a hospital as well as vicar of a parish. Sometimes he is at the hospital late on Saturday night, before a busy Sunday. Yet he offers himself "at any time of day or night" – and he means it. Such commitment from the rather undistinguished-looking church on the corner is more common than many people suppose.

We must stop there with the list incomplete. I am far from suggesting that Christians have a monopoly on social concern and action and I continue to be acutely aware of the Church's many failures. But I do pose this question. If there had been no Jesus Christ, and hence no Christian Church, would the world be any poorer?

Ask the workers of the last century; ask the homeless children; ask the slaves; ask those suffering from leprosy; ask the despairing; ask the homeless; ask the oppressed; ask the dying; ask ordinary parishioners.

And then ask yourself.

CONCLUDING QUOTATION

If the world is to be saved, it will be saved by the spirit. Politicians, or bankers, or soldiers, or businessmen, or even authors and artists are not the essential people. We need saints. The most relevant figures are not those who understand the world but those who can bring to the world something from outside itself, who can act as the transmitters of grace . . . God does not force humanity to survive, but at least we are sent enough saints in each generation to show us the possibility. A world guided by saints and the spirit would not only be a better world but also far, far safer into a much longer future – *Lord Rees-Mogg, in* The Independent, *21st December, 1992.*

TAKE A BREAK (2)
ALL ABOUT BISHOPS

Poor bishops! For the most part they are upright, intelligent men, who work very hard. Yet they are a favourite target for jokes, some of which – as you will see – are in rather poor taste! I thank Stuart Blanch – a retired archbishop – for not insisting that this page, or his Foreword, must go, and I ask all bishops, every-where, to forgive me. Fortunately, this is their Christian duty!

* * *

The bishop arrived to preach at Evensong, and he was disappointed at the turn-out. Rather annoyed, he questioned the vicar. "Didn't you tell them I was coming?" "No, my Lord", replied the hapless man, "but somehow the word seems to have got round."

A bishop was invited to the church fête, and the vicar talked to him about preaching. "Next Sunday I want to preach on humility. Can you recommend a good book on the subject?" The bishop pulled himself up to his full height. "There is only one," he replied, "and I wrote it."

*   *   *

There was an orderly queue at the pearly gates, when suddenly there was a loud fanfare of trumpets, and a great commotion. The gates opened, and an archbishop was rushed through in a huge Rolls-Royce. A little man near the front of the queue complained: "It's just the same in heaven as it was on earth; favouritism for the famous." The angel on duty laughed. "You've got it wrong, I'm afraid. Every day we let in thousands of ordinary people like you. But this is a day for celebration. We haven't admitted an archbishop for 300 years!"

*   *   *

This one's true (the last one wasn't, I promise). A bishop was conducting a large Communion service, and the public address system was playing up. He tapped the microphone, and said, "There's something wrong with this mike." But it was working well, and the vast congregation thought that the service had started. With one voice, they responded: "And also with you."

Part II

Questions about Science

Man is nothing but:
FAT enough for seven
   bars of soap

IRON enough for one
   medium-size nail

SUGAR enough for
   seven cups of tea

LIME enough to
   whitewash one
   chicken coop

MAGNESIUM
   enough for one dose
   of salts

PHOSPHOROUS
   enough to tip two
   thousand two
   hundred matches

POTASH enough to
   explode one toy
   crane

SULPHUR enough to
   rid one dog of fleas

Professor C. E. M. Joad

God does not play dice.

Albert Einstein

5

"But Surely, Sir, Science has Disproved God?"

The sentence which forms our chapter heading was addressed by a sixth-former to Professor Coulson, the late Oxford mathematician. The fact that the professor was not only a leading scientist, but also a Christian leader, was something which that student could not sort out. In suggesting that science and religion are opposed, he was speaking for a good many people.

In fact, the particular combination found in Dr. Coulson – scientist *and* Christian – has not been uncommon throughout the history of science.

Then . . . Many of the founders of modern science were men with a firm belief in God. Robert Boyle (1627–1691) and Sir Isaac Newton (1642–1727) are good examples.

Robert Boyle is well known for "Boyle's Law". Less well known is the fact that he wrote a book entitled *The Wisdom of God Manifested in the Works of Creation*. Newton has been called "the greatest scientist of all time". In addition to giving us his famous laws of motion, he contributed brilliantly to the fields of optics, astronomy, and that branch of mathematics called differential calculus. Yet Newton wrote theological as well as scientific books, and regarded his theological works as more important.

From a later period we may single out Michael Faraday (1791–1867) who discovered electromagnetism, and Sir James Young Simpson (1811–70), the first surgeon to use the anaesthetic properties of chloroform. In this way he paved the way for safe, painless surgery. So did Lord Joseph Lister (1827–1912) who pioneered antiseptic surgery, and saved thousands of lives and a great deal of suffering.

Each of these brilliant scientists had a deep personal faith. Simpson was asked to name his greatest discovery. He is reported to have replied, "It is not chloroform. My greatest discovery has been to know that I am a sinner and that I could be saved by the grace of God."

Louis Pasteur (1822–95), the French chemist who gave his name to pasteurised milk, is another distinguished example. So is Gregor Mendel (1822–84), whose researches into the laws of heredity form the basis of the modern science of genetics. Mendel was an Austrian monk, who became abbot of his monastery. The list goes on: James Clerk Maxwell, Lord Kelvin . . .

In seventeenth-century England the Royal Society – a gathering of leading scientists – dedicated its work "to the Glory of God the Creator, and the benefit of the human race". Two centuries later the British Association for the Advancement of Science held its first meeting in York. Those who gathered at that meeting in 1831 paid tribute to the Church, "without whose aid the Association would never have been founded". They went on to declare that "true religion and true science ever lead to the same great end". The Association's first two presidents were clergymen.

. . . and now: The scientist and Christian combination continues today. John Habgood – now Archbishop of York – was a research scientist. Several more professional scientists are convinced Christians, many of whom have written about the

relationships between science and Christianity: Tony Hewish, a radio astronomer and Nobel Prize winner; Arnold Wolfendale, Astronomer Royal since 1991, who said recently, "I think the hand of God can be seen everywhere"; Colin Humphrey, Professor of Metallurgy at Cambridge; Brian Heap, Director of the Animal Physiology and Genetics Research Institute and a Fellow of the Royal Society; Russell Stannard, Professor of Physics at the Open University and a lay preacher; Derek Burke, Vice-Chancellor of the University of East Anglia; Chris Isham, a cosmologist who is Professor at Imperial College, are distinguished examples from a much longer list. Christians in Science – a British organisation – has over 700 members. Its American counterpart has a membership of about 2,000.

So what? What is the significance of all this? It is not accidental that so many early scientists were men of strong Christian faith, and I will expand on this in Chapter 7. But at this stage I want to make clear what I am *not* saying.

By giving this impressive list of names, I am not trying to prove that Christianity is true. If every scientist in the world were a practising Christian it would not prove this. The evidence for Christianity is to be found mainly in the areas of *history* and *personal experience*, not in science – although the evidence is none the less impressive for that.

Not that all scientists *are* followers of Christ, of course; far from it. Convinced Christians are in a minority in every job (except ministers of churches, of course!). We would not expect to find a majority of scientists – nor bus drivers, dustmen or teachers – to be believers. And it is well known that some scientists have recorded their *dis*-belief in Christianity.

The list of distinguished names does not prove that Christianity is true. What it *does* show is that Christianity and science are not opposed. The sixth-former was wrong. *For if two teams really are competing against each other, no key player can be on both sides at the same time.* And because scientists are intelligent people, the fact that a fair number of scientists are Christians also suggests that Christianity is not just a fairy story, suitable only for those who cannot think for themselves.

If it is true that Christianity and science are not opposed, why do so many people think that they are? The seeds of this distortion were sown in two famous conflicts, and we shall consider these. But there are other factors, too. For one thing, unlike so many of the *founders* of modern science, several later *popularisers* of science were militant atheists. They spread their beliefs with missionary zeal.

Their atheism did not arise directly from scientific investigation, although they sometimes gave this impression. By the time they spread their views, scientific method was firmly established. Science was able to cut free from its Christian origins, and develop a life of its own. God appeared to be redundant.

This view has been reinforced by some modern scientists who vigorously express their conviction that God does not exist. They believe that the universe is without ultimate meaning or purpose. Some assert that the "chance" factor which operates in sub-atomic physics lends support to their beliefs.

These views are strongly opposed by scientists who are Christians. To them, the vastness of space, the complexity of matter, and the elegant simplicity of the basic mathematics "behind" it all, point to the marvellous mind of the Maker. But the "science versus religion" controversy is seen at its sharpest in two famous incidents. Two names sum it up: Galileo and Darwin.

Galileo and the heresy trial

The brilliant Italian astronomer Galileo Galilei (1564–1642) was persecuted by the Church of his day for arguing that the earth is not at the centre of the universe. It was not a question of an atheist fighting against the Christians. Galileo was a devout Catholic who believed in God just as much as the Church leaders. It was a clash between two views about authority, and the correct approach to truth.

Of course, this doesn't excuse the Church leaders for their blind attitude and appalling actions. But it is worth noting that many of Galileo's closest friends and strongest supporters were clergy. Also significant is the fact that Galileo was building on the work of Nicolaus Copernicus (1473–1543). Copernicus laid the foundation for the scientific revolution by suggesting – on mathematical grounds – that the earth travels round the sun. He held office in the Polish Church as a canon of Frauenburg Cathedral. Copernicus described God as "the Best and Most Orderly Workman of all".

Charles Darwin and evolution

In 1859 Charles Darwin published his book *The Origin of Species by Means of Natural Selection*. He put forward the view that life on earth has evolved into higher and higher forms over a long period. But the early chapters of Genesis seem to give a different explanation. We read there that God created the world in six days. It seemed that if Darwin was right, the Bible must be wrong. There was an almighty rumpus.

As with the Galileo controversy, it is significant to notice how the opponents lined up. Some scientists (e.g., Richard Owen, a leading biologist) ridiculed Darwin's theory. In contrast, some Christians (e.g., the clergyman Charles Kingsley, and F. J. A. Hort, a distinguished Cambridge theologian) welcomed Darwin's researches in the name of truth. But some other churchmen, notably Bishop Samuel Wilberforce, attacked Darwin. A lasting – and false – impression was given. Popular history records the event as "the Church *versus* Evolution". Game, set and match to evolution.

It is interesting to notice where Charles Darwin himself stood. Because of the controversy caused by his *Origin of Species* and *Descent of Man*, he is often thought to be a great enemy of the Christian Faith. It is true that he wrote, "I gradually came to disbelieve in Christianity as a divine revelation". But he spoke about "The Creator" and used a quotation which spoke of the need to study "God's word" and "God's works".

Lord Tennyson, the poet, asked Darwin whether his theory of evolution attacked Christianity, and Darwin replied, "No, certainly not."

Darwin's attitude to missionary work is interesting. Early in his career he travelled widely on HMS *Beagle*, undertaking scientific research. During the five-year voyage his ship visited Tierra del Fuego, at the southern tip of South America. Darwin knew, from personal observation, that the inhabitants of that island were very primitive. When he heard that Christian missionaries were going there, he thought that they were bound to fail. He was wrong, and he was humble enough to admit it. In 1870 he wrote to the South American Missionary Society – an Anglican society which continues to do great work today:

> The success of the Tierra del Fuego Mission is most wonderful, and charms me, as I always prophesied utter failure. It is a grand success. I shall feel proud if your committee think fit to elect me an honorary member of your society.

And so we find Charles Darwin, eleven years after the publication of his most controversial book, in the unexpected role of supporter of Christian missionary work. He did not become a Christian believer, but in this way he acknowledged the excellent work of the missionaries, and the effectiveness of Christianity in action.

What then of Genesis?

"In the beginning God created the heavens and the earth . . ." These opening verses of the Bible were read to the world by the Apollo 8 team as they circled the moon on Christmas Day 1968. If it is true that the argument between science and Christianity has lost its heat, how has it been resolved? In particular, what are we to make of those chapters in Genesis which describe the creation of the world? It was these passages which were at the centre of the controversy.

This is one of those areas where we find a variety of opinions among Christians. This was demonstrated very clearly in 1985 by the publication of a book designed as a forum for debate on this question. The book, entitled *Creation and Evolution* (Editor: Derek Burke), has eight contributors, most of whom are distinguished scientists. They were carefully chosen to ensure that a wide range of opinions emerged. Some of them contest views held by most scientists, for example about the age of our earth. Their discussion is too complex to summarise, but I set out below three viewpoints which are most commonly expressed on this issue today.

1. Some maintain that the early chapters in Genesis should be taken literally. As far as they are concerned, the battle is still on. If the theory of evolution appears to clash with the Bible, so much the worse for the theory of evolution. They point out that some philosophers (e.g. Karl Popper) criticise the theory as not being truly scientific, and that Darwin's views have been considerably modified by later scientists.

Verna Wright is a former Professor of Rheumatology at Leeds University. In *Creation and Evolution* he writes:

> For myself I believe in a six-day creation. A straight-forward reading of Genesis by an intelligent man, not exposed to the evolutionary model, would suggest a literal six-day creation. The only way around this interpretation would be to suggest the account was allegorical or poetic. Neither in the opening chapters of Genesis nor elsewhere in the Bible is there a suggestion that the account is symbolic. Moreover, it is not found in the poetic section of the Old Testament.

He goes on to remind us that the Ten Commandments contain the phrase "for in six days the Lord made heaven and earth". He adds: "With respect, it is worth reminding ourselves that it was the Creator himself who was speaking." Views held by a professional scientist, on a subject which he has studied closely, must be weighed carefully.

2. Many Christians strongly disagree with this approach. Some believe that this insistence on "Special Creation" hampers evangelism – drawing the attention of non-believers away from Jesus and onto sterile secondary issues. They are worried that unbelievers will write off the Church as "anti-science", and shut their ears to the claims of Christ.

They point out that astronomers speak of the vast age of the universe (the "big bang" took place some 15,000 million years ago, and events of momentous significance occurred in the first three minutes, according to current theory). They note, too, that despite modifications to Darwin's theory, the majority of biologists think that there are good grounds for accepting evolution.

As a result, they maintain that it is quite possible to accept the theory of evolution *and* the Bible. The Bible tells us *that* God created the world and all living creatures; scientific theories like evolution attempt to tell us *how* he did it. They may go on to point out that the order of creation in Genesis 1 is similar to that suggested by scientists investigating the origins of life on earth (e.g., water creatures before land creatures). They may suggest that the six "days" of creation in Genesis represent very long periods of time.

3.   Other Christians agree broadly with this view, but argue that even the points about order and time are not really important. They maintain that it is essential to view the early chapters of Genesis as *pre*-scientific or *non*-scientific literature. They were written centuries before the rise of modern science. Whether or not they square with the findings of scientists is therefore unimportant, for the author – or editor(s) – was not concerned with modern scientific questions.

The description of the Creation in Genesis, and theories developed within modern science, do not *agree* or *disagree* with each other, because they use different types of language and are concerned with different problems. Dr. Alan Richardson expressed this viewpoint when he said that Genesis "is dealing with matters beyond the scope of science".

Central to these last two views is the idea that *literal* truth is not the only *real* truth. We are, of course, quite used to accepting statements as true, even though we would not dream of taking them literally.

I lost my head	She's an old battle-axe
I smell a rat	He's got a frog in his throat
Get your act together	I jumped out of my skin

When Robert Burns wrote "O my Luve's like a red, red rose" we understand that he did not mean that every embrace was extremely painful. Nor that his girlfriend's complexion suggested that she was prone to nosebleeds!

The Bible often uses vivid picture language of this kind. I doubt that the Psalmist really saw the hills clapping their hands, or skipping like lambs. And St. Peter reminds us that in God's eyes, one day and one thousand years amount to the same thing (2 Pet. 3:8).

The same principle applies to the parables of Jesus. Did the Prodigal Son or the Good Samaritan exist outside the imagination of Jesus? Did he *really* know of a widow who pestered a judge, or a woman who lost a coin? Perhaps; perhaps not. It simply does not matter. We would not accuse Jesus of lying if he invented those characters to illustrate the truths he wanted to communicate. To do so would be like refusing to take a novel seriously because the characters are fictitious! Parables and novels can convey profound truths without being *literally* true.

The same approach can be applied to the early chapters of Genesis. We can believe that the accounts of the Creation were inspired by God, without maintaining that Genesis is intended to give a literal, scientifically exact account of the way in which the world began. We must not judge it as though this were the intention.

But it is true. It teaches vitally important truths about God, about us, and about the world in which we live.

God created the world. Human beings are the "crown" of God's creation. We were given freedom and responsibility. The first human beings rebelled against God, and this rebellion affected the subsequent history of the world. All these truths are found in those first few chapters of the Bible. They are expressed there with a superb, poetic artistry which can be understood by people of all ages and cultures.

But Genesis doesn't only give us a history lesson. With clear insight it focuses our own personal conflicts. We see mirrored in Adam and Eve our own personal fall from innocence; our own struggles with temptation; our own fears; our own corruption; our own self-deception; our own desire to wriggle out of responsibility for our actions. (Adam said it was Eve's fault; Eve quickly passed the parcel to the serpent. Only yesterday I caught myself at the same game!)

On the basis of reading the first few chapters of Genesis and taking them seriously but not literally, what sort of world would we expect to find? We should expect a world in which there is a great deal of beauty and design, *plus* a great deal of trouble and disharmony. In short, we would expect to find the world *as it actually is*.

This is the genius of the book of Genesis. It describes and explains the human situation in a most profound way. The glory and the tragedy are both there. Genesis raises deep questions about our relationship with God, with nature, and with other people. The rest of the Bible shows the solution to these vital questions being worked out in the lives of individuals and nations.

Such literature is every bit as important as a scientific treatise on the origins of the universe.

CONCLUDING QUOTATION

In *Doing Away with God?* physics professor Russell Stannard, who is also a lay preacher, wrote:

> I earnestly look forward to the day when it will be generally recognized that one can take on board all the deep truths of the Genesis creation stories, *and in addition*, the scientific truths about God's world. Then we shall see how God is revealing himself through this Big Bang world of ours. He is actually speaking to us through these scientific discoveries.

He goes on to suggest that the immensity of space and time speak of God's majesty, power, patience and ingenuity. His book is well worth reading.

6

More about Christianity and Science

There are basically three ways of viewing the relationship between science and Christianity. The "antagonistic view" suggests that science has disproved religion, and we examined that in the previous chapter. In this chapter we consider two other views.

1. God is in there somewhere

Some Christians, knowing that scientists are explaining more and more, look anxiously for gaps in scientific knowledge. They search for unanswered scientific questions and assert that God is at work in these gaps in a way which is beyond scientific explanation. In this way they hope to defend the existence of God in a scientific age. We cannot do without God, they maintain, for the gaps in scientific knowledge can only be accounted for by his direct activity. For obvious reasons, this view is sometimes called "the God of the gaps". It is a fatal approach for two reasons:

a) The gaps in scientific knowledge are still enormous, but they are shrinking all the time. What was a large gap ten years ago may be a very small gap, or no gap at all, now. Hence God appears to be squeezed out.

b) This view is based on a false understanding of the relationship between God and his Creation. The Bible teaches that God is "behind" or "upholds" the *whole* of Creation, not just the puzzling parts. He is every bit as responsible for those areas which *can* be explained by scientists, as those which (as yet, anyway) *cannot*.

This defensive view, or God of the gaps, is as false as the antagonistic view.

2. Two ways of looking at the same thing

This is by far the most satisfactory approach to the problem. Christianity and science view and explain things from two *different*, but *equally valid*, angles.

One common way of expressing this is to say that science asks *how?* questions (*how* does this work?), while religion asks *why?* questions. This oversimplifies the position but it remains a useful distinction. (The fact that deep *why?* questions are asked by ordinary people was brought home to me by a young child. She turned thoughtfully from looking out of a window and asked: "Why is there anything at all?" Those in the know will recall that the philosopher Martin Heidegger posed the same question: "Why is there something, and not nothing?")

A few everyday examples will illustrate the principle behind this approach.

People: A newspaper article suggested that Miss World is in reality a collection of chemicals, costing a few pounds. We see from this the importance of taking more than one viewpoint into account. And it shows the danger of phrases like "nothing but", "only", "merely" and "nothing more than".

Miss World, like the rest of us, *is* made up of chemicals. But she is not *only* or *nothing but* a mixture of chemicals. Ask the television audience! It is perfectly valid to view human beings from the point of view of their chemical composition. It is *not* valid to suggest that this is the only viewpoint which matters.

Similarly, it can be useful – and accurate – to think of a person as a machine, or as an advanced animal, or as a walking computer. The fatal mistake is to think that by describing him in these ways, we rule out other viewpoints – a spiritual viewpoint for example. To say that human beings are animals ("naked apes") is one thing. To say that we are *nothing but* animals is something quite different.

Objects: Any object can be viewed from a variety of viewpoints which complement, or add to, one another. For example, a diamond may be regarded by a millionaire as an article giving prestige, by a geologist as a piece of native crystallised carbon with a hardness of 10, and by an engaged couple as a symbol of their love. To ask which single viewpoint is the right one shows a lack of understanding. *Each* of them is correct.

Events: Events can be explained from different viewpoints as well. They can be described in *scientific* terms and in *personal* terms.

A window is broken. Why?

Answer in scientific terms: When a missile weighing four ounces, and travelling at 60 miles per hour, strikes a pane of glass 2mm thick, the glass will shatter.

Answer in personal terms: Johnny Green has made a catapult.

Johnny Green is crying. Why?

Answer in scientific terms: When a missile the weight of a man's hand, travelling at 40 miles per hour, strikes the skin, the nerve ends are aggravated.

Answer in personal terms: Johnny Green's dad was so wild when he received the bill for a new window that he slapped his son's rump with considerable vigour.

To ask which of these explanations is correct is clearly absurd. It is not a question of either/or. We have two completely different explanations and *both are correct*.

Of course, one of the explanations may be more *appropriate* to the situation than the other. If you had given Johnny's dad the scientific explanation to his angry question about the broken window, he would have been even more angry! But both explanations are true, even though only one is sufficiently relevant to be worth stating.

This principle applies to everything. Why is the kettle boiling? When the temperature of water is raised to 100° Celsius (at standard pressure), rapid evaporation takes place. Why is the kettle boiling? It is 4 o'clock, and old Mrs. Brown always makes a cup of tea at that time. And so we could go on. But we must return to the central question. What has this to do with science and religion?

God and Nature: What applies to everyday events – the broken window, the boiling kettle – can be applied to really big events as well.

Why does the earth support life? It is quite possible to give an answer in scientific terms. Factors like the importance of carbon, and the size of the earth being just right to support an atmosphere, will be mentioned. But it is equally possible to give an explanation in "personal" terms – by maintaining that these factors express God's good and fruitful purpose. If this is the case, then scientists are discovering the way in which God has designed the world. By doing so they help us to see his greatness.

Hence Sir James Jeans could speak of God as a mathematician, and Kepler, the brilliant early astronomer, could say that he was "thinking God's thoughts after Him". Dr. Malcolm Dixon, a biochemist, put it clearly. "If we believe that God made the world, have we the slightest ground for saying that He did not do it through the operation of natural laws and natural forces? . . . Surely not."

It is, of course, open to anyone to disagree with the explanation in terms of the activity of God. Others may wish to explain the universe as the result of chance, not as the work of God. But it is *not* open to anyone to disagree with the explanation in terms of God just *because* science can explain how the earth supports life.

The fact that science can give an explanation does not, and cannot, disprove the explanation in personal terms. To suggest this is like arguing that the scientific explanation for Johnny

Green's stinging bottom proves that his father did not spank him! The two explanations are complementary. They stand side by side and fit together.

To sum up: scientists – *as* scientists – cannot comment on whether God is "behind" the universe or not, because this is not a scientific question. As thoughtful human beings they will, of course, have views on this matter. Science does not and cannot disprove religion. Nor does it prove religion to be true. Science and religion look at the universe from different viewpoints, and ask different sets of important questions.

CONCLUDING QUOTATION

It is the contention of the Christian that, in order to do full justice to the totality of his experience, he finds it necessary to see and interpret the over-all pattern of his experience not only in biochemical, physiological or psychological terms, but also in religious terms – *Malcolm Jeeves, former Professor of Psychology at St. Andrew's University.*

TAKE A BREAK (3)

Confessions by the author (all true, I promise!)
As a young curate, my ministry got off to a rather bad start. My local paper reported that I would be working at St. Dude's. An excusable mistake no doubt; St. Jude isn't the best known of saints, and I confess that I did feel rather like a Dude, in my brand-new dog collar.

*   *   *

Then there was the youth club. I sauntered in – rather like a Dude, I suppose – and casually picked up a table-tennis bat. Soon I was playing a hard match, and trying desperately to impress.

At the first opportunity I made an exotic smash. Then the trouble began. My fast-moving arm hit a bystander who was drinking a bottle of coke. Result: one youth club member was minus one tooth.

He was very understanding and he freely forgave me.

Fortunately, one of the church lay-readers was an excellent dentist. Some years later, when I was working at a college in Sussex, a new student introduced herself. "Bob Mills is our church youth club leader," she said. "He sends greetings, and he still forgives you for knocking out his tooth!"

* * *

The table-tennis incident was followed by further embarrassment. We were voting for PCC members. Whether or not curates should vote, I don't know, but I did. On my ballot paper I listed all the names, then crossed them out as I put them in rank order. Result: one very scruffy voting paper.

When the ballot was over, a small group was asked to go to another room to count the votes. As we counted, one of my colleagues stopped with a snort. "Really," she exclaimed, "some of our people are almost illiterate." To prove her point she passed round my voting paper. To my shame, I looked at it, agreed with her, and passed it on.

7

Common Ground

We have noted some of the differences between science and religion, but it is important to observe that they share some common ground. I will mark out four areas.

1. How science began

At this point, I invite you to take part in the world's shortest questionnaire. Please tick a, b or c.

   a) Without Jesus there would be no modern science.

   b) Nonsense: Jesus had nothing to do with the rise of science.

   c) The answer lies somewhere between a) and b).

No Jesus; no science! This provocative statement *could* be right. We can't prove it, of course – because we cannot imagine what the world would be like without his immense influence. But the actual truth is almost as startling. *Christian faith gave birth to modern science.*

This isn't my own cranky personal view. For example, the historian Herbert Butterfield affirmed that science is a child of Christian thought. The philosophers A. N. Whitehead and John MacMurray made the same point. MacMurray affirmed that "Science is the legitimate child of a great religious movement, and its genealogy goes back to Jesus."

Those who take this view emphasise that science could only get under way when certain factors were present. One of the most important ingredients was the correct mental approach. For true science to develop it was vital that certain beliefs about the nature of the world should be widespread. The belief that:
- matter is essentially good
- the same laws apply everywhere
- human beings are called to be stewards of creation
- time moves forward in a straight line, rather than round in circles

These views are expounded in the Bible. In contrast, some religions teach that matter is evil, or that we should be detached from the world, or that different gods rule different aspects of life, or that time goes round in endless cycles.

Some ancient Greeks and medieval Arabs were very good at mathematics, and deeply interested in scientific questions. There were important advances. But in the event, it was Christian civilisation which brought science to birth. The early scientists realised that they must *look* and *investigate* if they were to discover the laws which God has ordained. It seems so obvious, but it was a crucial breakthrough in approach.

Dr. Peter Hodgson, Lecturer in Nuclear Physics at Oxford University, puts it this way: "Christianity provided just those beliefs that are essential for science, and the whole moral climate that encouraged its growth."

2. Science and religion need each other

Science – and its offspring, technology – have transformed our world. The spectacular success of science over the last three hundred years has given it massive authority. Religion, too, continues to make a considerable impact on individuals and societies – sometimes, alas, for ill rather than for good. But at their best, the world's many religions spread love, justice and understanding.

Science and religion need each other. To give one example: the energetic drive to arrest leprosy has been spearheaded by Christians. This campaign of compassion is based on obedience to the call of Jesus (Matt. 10:8) *and* on the techniques of modern medical skill.

But scientific discoveries can be used for good or ill. The dark shadows cast by germ and nuclear warfare are chilling reminders of this. In medicine and genetics, impressive new techniques present complex ethical questions (consider *Jurassic Park*!). Our troubled and divided world needs wisdom, compassion and sensitivity, as never before.

Christians don't claim a monopoly on these qualities. But if the Christian Faith is true, they should be in evidence in the community of believers – and readily available for use in our world of dangerous tension and difficult decision-making.

3. Science and religion both put limits on "commonsense"

As a Londoner living in Yorkshire I have come to value commonsense. There's a lot of it about in these parts! We are right to place a high value upon it, for it is another word for practical wisdom, or good decision-making.

But science sounds a warning bell about commonsense. Recently I stood on a cliff-top. It jutted out, and as I looked at the sea on three sides, two things were quite clear. First, the earth is flat. Second, if I ventured near the edge of that saucer-shaped horizon, I should fall off. That was the verdict of commonsense.

The verdict of science – that I was standing on a sphere from which I could not fall, even if I wanted to – seemed very far-fetched. But I accept that verdict, not the verdict of my eyes.

Shortly after that day out, I heard a radio programme on

science and religion. The scientists agreed that they often have to ignore or press beyond, the commonsense "obvious" explanation. A stone might appear to be solid. Look "closer" and you are dealing with empty space, and packets of energy.

One of those scientists was a Christian, and he discussed the question of paradox. He noted that for decades scientists had to live with two irreconcilable views of the nature of light. One set of data told them that light is made up of a stream of particles. Other evidence told them that light is a series of waves. About one thing they were clear: it couldn't be both! But in 1928 a scientist solved this puzzle. Paul Dirac invented quantum field theory, which is able to integrate all the information.

That scientist went on to say that Christianity sometimes challenges commonsense in the same kind of way. How can God be three in one? How could Jesus be both God and man? In his view, such puzzles have the ring of reality about them. He certainly didn't want to hide behind mysteries. But as a scientist he is used to finding surprises when he is dealing with deep questions at the limits of our understanding.

Christianity does not require us to believe six impossible things before breakfast. But – like science – it sometimes asks us to be adventurous enough to cope with surprises, and to question "obvious" everyday beliefs.

4. Science and Christianity both acknowledge limitations

The whole purpose of scientific activity is to press back the frontiers of knowledge; to replace ignorance by understanding. Most religions are involved in a similar quest – though the questions they put are different from scientific questions. Why are we here? What happens when we die? Is there purpose in life? Does God exist? How can we cope with evil within our own hearts and lives? These are questions with which the Christian Faith grapples – questions which ultimately face us all.

Science and Christianity both ask questions in an attitude of humility. At least, their best practitioners do. St. Paul summed up the Christian position like this: "Now we see but a poor reflection as in a mirror; then we shall see face to face. Now I know in part; then I shall know fully, even as I am fully known" (1 Cor. 13:12). Ancient mirrors gave an imperfect reflection; total clarity was rare. This is St. Paul's point.

We *do* have light by which to live. Christians believe that this light shines at its brightest in the person of Jesus. But there are many answers to the riddles of life at which we can only guess.

God deals with us in a very practical manner. Our curiosity is great, and we should like light on a whole range of questions. Instead, God gives us just enough to be getting on with. We are like people with a powerful torch on a dark night. The torch lights up the path, but it doesn't enable us to see the surrounding countryside. One day, however, we shall see the whole majestic view, in the light of eternity.

In the same way, modern scientists know that their understanding is limited. In earlier centuries, some scientists believed that nature would inevitably yield all her secrets to their investigations. In these days of quarks, gluons and black holes in space, they acknowledge "that nature is now seen to be mysterious; much of it is unknown, unknowable and unfathomable."

Those words were written by Professor Harold Schilling, a distinguished American physicist. Dr. Lewis Thomas, another scientist, makes the same point: "We do not understand much of anything . . . we have a wilderness of mystery to make our way through in the centuries ahead." Others put this more positively, preferring "inexhaustible riches" to "wilderness of mystery".

CONCLUDING QUOTATIONS

Science without religion is lame, religion without science is blind – *Albert Einstein, who revolutionised modern physics with his Theory of Relativity.*

Religion and natural science are fighting a joint battle in an incessant, never relaxing crusade against scepticism and against dogmatism, against disbelief and against superstition, and the rallying cry in this crusade has always been, and always will be: "On to God" – *Max Planck, awarded the Nobel Prize for his work on the Quantum Theory.*

Science brings man nearer to God – *Louis Pasteur, who revolutionised microbiology.*

Historically, religion came first and science grew out of religion. Science has never superseded religion, and it is my expectation that it never will supersede it – *the eminent historian Arnold Toynbee.*

*　　*　　*

Note: the four areas discussed in this chapter by no means cover all the common ground between science and religion. For example, recent authors have drawn attention to the importance of faith and intuition in science; to the fact that modern scientific activity is often corporate (indeed, international) in nature; and to the sense of awe and wonder sometimes evoked by the scientific investigation.

8

A Short Chapter about a Long Climb

In 1961 Yuri Gagarin became the first human being in space. On his return to earth, it was widely reported that he had not seen God "up there". This naive assertion still rumbles, and it deserves a naive reply. No doubt Yuri G. spoke with tongue in cheek – which is how I am writing.

When I broadcast the following "parable" on local radio, it seemed to catch the imagination. It was selected for *Pick of the Week* on Radio 4, and I received letters and phone calls requesting a copy. In view of this, I decided to include this little tale as a "fun" postscript to the hard work of the previous three chapters. When broadcast it was adorned by Scott Joplin's "The Entertainer". Alas, modern technology is as yet unable to reproduce this music from the printed page.

Perhaps I should add that the original, excellent, idea wasn't mine. Sadly, I don't know whose idea it was; it came to my notice as an aside in a long-forgotten conversation. But the parable itself is my handiwork; I alone am to blame!

*   *   *

Once upon a time there lived a community of mice. They lived in a large house, and their front door was a hole in the skirting board of the music room. In the music room there was a grand piano, and from time to time they heard beautiful music.

"Ah," they would say. "Beautiful," they would sigh. But sometimes the music stirred debate. Deep debate. There was a piano – of that they were sure. And there was beautiful music – of that they were sure, too. But . . . *was there a musician?*

Some were quite certain. "Stuff and nonsense" said the atheists. "If we could see inside the piano we should understand how music is made. All this talk of design and intention is quite unnecessary."

"Stuff and nonsense," said the believing mice. "You are quite wrong. Beautiful music like that certainly doesn't happen by chance. If there is music, there must be a musician." "Stuff and nonsense," said the agnostic mice. "We simply don't have enough evidence to decide one way or the other. We are in the dark and we shall remain in the dark. Get on with sharing the cheese."

Within the community there was one especially curious mouse called – yes, you've guessed it – Michael. One day he decided to go on an adventure of discovery. He would settle this question; and he would settle it *now*.

He crept to the hole in the skirting board, and began to climb the leg of the grand piano. When he was halfway up, the beautiful music started again. With the greatest difficulty he climbed the shiny sheer surface. He was bursting with curiosity. Just what would he see?

At last he completed his climb and peered inside. He looked, he gasped, and he scampered down the leg, across the floor and back through the hole in the wall. As he returned the entire community gathered around. "What did you see?" they demanded, in great excitement.

"I climbed the leg of the piano," panted Michael, "and I looked inside the piano . . . and I saw how music is made!"

There was a deep silence. Michael caught his breath and he continued, "I saw lots of little wooden hammers striking lots of metal wires . . . *I saw . . . no pianist.*"

That night, as they went to bed, some were jubilant. They had been proved right. The pianist was a myth; a figment of the imagination. Others had mixed feelings. It was good to know the truth, but they were disappointed just the same. Others were downright sad. It wasn't simply that they had been proved wrong. It was bigger than that. Life was rather less interesting than they had hoped, and much more empty. It seemed that, after all, there really was nothing more to do than to get on with sharing and eating the cheese.

CONCLUDING QUOTATION

The laws of nature have to be just right to allow stars like our sun to burn steadily as a long-term source of energy. Without that reliability the development of life on earth would have been impossible. The stars are also the nuclear furnaces in which carbon and the other raw materials of life are formed. We are all made from the ashes of dead stars. That is only possible because the nuclear forces are "finely-tuned" to allow this to happen. Life is not possible in "any old world"; it requires a universe in a trillion – *John Polkinghorne.*

Part III

Questions about the Bible

The existence of the Bible is the greatest blessing which humanity ever experienced.

Immanuel Kant

A multi-million-pound con-job.

Anonymous

Men turn this way and that in their search for new sources of comfort and inspiration, but the enduring truths are to be found in the word of God.

Queen Elizabeth the Queen Mother

9

You Can't Believe the Bible Today

A friend of mine conducted some street interviews for local radio. On one occasion his subject was the Bible. One person dismissed it as "a multi-million-pound con-job". This extreme response wasn't common, but it became clear that many people feel very unsure about the reliability of the Bible.

A best-seller? Certainly. Interesting? Possibly. But when it comes to the really important question of *truth* – more fiction than fact.

If they are right, this is extremely damaging to the Christian Faith, for we are largely dependent upon the New Testament for our information about Jesus. This is the only place where we find anything like a full account of his ministry.

Certainly, it is a less detailed account than we might wish. But – the crucial question – is it an *accurate* account? Christianity demands that we should drastically alter our lives. In return, we are right to demand that it should produce strong credentials.

A: BASED ON ACCURATE RECORDS?

The procedure for assessing the reliability of the New Testament is the same as for any other important ancient document, when the original no longer exists. There are two vital factors, both of which depend on the discovery of copies of the original.

The first factor involves the *number* of copies which have been found. The second concerns the *age* of these copies – the time lag between the original document and the copies which now exist.

We can be confident that we possess an accurate record when (1) we find several copies which are basically similar, and (2) the copies we have are fairly near in time to the original author.

A time span which seems great to us will satisfy the experts, provided there are enough copies to enable them to cross-check. (Provided, also, that these copies were not all taken from the same earlier copy.) Here is a table which compares the four Gospels with some other famous ancient manuscripts.

In order to get the strength of the evidence for the Gospels, I invite you to put your own estimates in the spaces marked with an asterisk in the diagram. We shall consider the bottom line (D) first.

1. How many?

It proved difficult to find an accurate figure for the number of existing ancient hand-written copies of the Gospels in Greek – the language in which they were originally written. To solve the problem I wrote to Tyndale House in Cambridge – a centre which specialises in Biblical research.

They could not give me an accurate figure either, for the list is too long to count without taking a very long time! For copies

Ancient Writing	Thucy-dides' HISTORY	Caesar's GALLIC WAR	Tacitus' HISTORIES	The Four Gospels
(A) Date of original document	460–400 BC	58–50 BC	AD 100	AD 65–90
(B) Oldest surviving copy	AD 900 (plus a few 1st century fragments)	AD 850	AD 800	*
(C) Approx. time between A and B	1300 years (fragments 400 years)	900 years	700 years	*
(D) Number of ancient copies in existence today	8	10	2	*

made before AD 1000 they suggested that I should use the phrase "many hundreds, hundreds upon hundreds". Compare this with 8, 10 and 2, and you can see that the Gospels are in a different league altogether.

2. How long?

Now to the time factor. There are two existing copies of the New Testament dated AD 350 – less than three hundred years after the original. This compares very favourably with the 1300, 900, and 700 years for the other books listed in the chart (see row C). One of these very old copies of the New Testament is in the Vatican Library. The other is in the British Museum. The British

Government bought it from the Soviet Government on Christmas Day 1933, for £100,000 – a tremendous bargain! (Russia continues to hold – in Leningrad – the oldest surviving complete copy of the Hebrew Scriptures, apart from the Dead Sea Scrolls.)

When we take into account *incomplete copies* of the New Testament, the situation is even more impressive – a few excellent manuscripts are 100 to 200 years earlier still. Some of the Chester Beatty and Bodmer Papyri are dated before AD 250. Each of these contains copies of the Gospels. The Bodmer copy of St. John was made as early as AD 200 and contains about two-thirds of the complete Gospel. The earliest discovery of all is a fragment from John's Gospel. It is dated at a breathtaking AD 130 (see page 106).

Incomplete documents are found because portions of some manuscripts were destroyed or lost, and also because scribes sometimes copied only one section of the New Testament. Start copying all twenty-seven books and you will see why!

Summary

As with the number, so with the time gap: the evidence for the Gospels is streets ahead of other ancient documents. No one doubts that we have a reliable text of Caesar's Gallic War and the rest. The case for the reliability of the New Testament is far stronger.

I will call on Bishop John Robinson to sum up. He is a particularly interesting witness because of his radical credentials. His book *Honest to God* sold millions of copies around the world, and showed that he was not afraid to rock the boat.

His much better book *Can We Trust the New Testament?* has sold far fewer copies, probably because of its much more orthodox conclusions. But his conclusions do not arise from a loss of nerve. Up to his untimely death from cancer in 1984, he continued to follow the argument wherever the evidence led him. This is what he said on the subject under discussion:

To return to the textual transmission of the New Testament, the wealth of manuscripts, and above all the narrow interval of time between the writing and the earliest extant copies, make it by far the best-attested text of any ancient writing in the world.

He also draws on the Oxford classical historian, A. N. Sherwin-White, who "chides New Testament scholars for failing to recognise what by any comparable standards excellent sources they have!"

This view is shared by other scholars: "There is much more evidence for the New Testament than for other ancient writings of comparable date" (F. F. Bruce). "In spite of the numerous possibilities for error, the New Testament is probably the most trustworthy piece of writing that has survived from antiquity" (M. C. Tenney). "The New Testament manuscripts in our possession are much closer in time to the original writings, more numerous and in closer agreement with each other than any other ancient book" (Hans Küng).

B: BASED ON ACCURATE MEMORIES?

We can be confident, then, about modern translations of the New Testament. They are based on ancient documents which faithfully record what St. Mark and the others wrote. But can we also be sure that the Gospel writers accurately recorded the life and death of Jesus in the first place?

This apparently straightforward question leads us into a minefield of dispute! According to some theologians the question itself is misleading. They assert that the four Gospels are concerned with theology, not history. On this view Matthew, Mark, Luke and John were much more interested in the question, *"What is the significance of Jesus?"* than with the question *"What did Jesus do and say?"*

Other theologians disagree. They believe that the Evangelists were interested in *both* these questions, for an event and its significance – history and theology – belong together. No event, no significance! But it has sometimes been left to experts in ancient history and literature, not theology, to insist on the overall historical reliability of the Gospels.

Having weighed the various issues, I continue to be convinced that four questions take us to the heart of the matter.

1. *Could* they have invented the material?

Jesus lived in the public eye from about AD 27 to AD 30, when he was crucified. The Gospels are very largely concerned with those three years.

Mark's Gospel was probably the first to be completed – by about AD 65. It is likely that large parts of Matthew and Luke – especially those parts which record the teaching of Jesus – were written down by AD 50, some twenty years after his death.

This seems a long time until we remember that the early Christians were much less concerned than we are with writing, and much more concerned with speaking and memorising. Even today, some Muslims memorise the entire Qur'ān – their Holy Book. It is shorter than the Bible, but substantial none the less. No wonder Professor Nineham could write about "the wonderfully retentive memory of the Oriental".

In the days of Jesus, disciples often remembered by rote the teachings of their rabbis. To help them, the rabbis sometimes cast their teachings in poetic form. Jesus certainly did. This can be seen when passages in the Greek New Testament are translated back into Aramaic, the "native" language of Jesus.

Stories were told, and sermons were preached about Jesus from the moment he died. They were written down only when those who had been with him during his life began to run the risk of death, either from persecution or from natural causes. It was rather like a modern lecturer making a book out of the things which he and his colleagues have been saying in their lectures for several years.

A man who was twenty when Jesus was crucified would have been about forty when the teaching material used by Matthew and Luke was written down and circulated – and about fifty-five when Mark completed his account. Indeed, he may have been younger than that. For in *Redating the New Testament* John Robinson argues that the Gospels – and other New Testament books – were written earlier than is commonly supposed.

Thousands heard Jesus teach, and saw him in action. Thousands more heard the preaching about him from the time of his death. If one of the preachers had radically altered the account, there would have been an outcry – from friends and enemies. If the material when written down had been very different from the preaching of the early disciples, a similar protest would have followed.

The fact that there were plenty of eye-witnesses does not guarantee every item in the Gospels, but it does guarantee their *general* reliability. Winston Churchill did great things during the Second World War, but if someone now suggested that he had healed the sick or miraculously fed the crowds, the balloon would soon go up! The span of time since the war is longer than the gap between Jesus and the written record about him.

Another point is raised by the question, "Could the early preachers, or the Gospel writers, have invented the teaching of Jesus?" Quite literally – *could* they? Or are the sayings so majestic that only someone as great as Jesus could have uttered them?

Beverley Nichols made this point very forcibly some years ago.

You cannot deny the reality of this character, *in whatever body it resided* . . . *somebody* said, "The Sabbath was made for man, and not man for the Sabbath"; *somebody* said, "For what shall it profit a man if he shall gain the whole world and lose his own soul"; *somebody* said, "Suffer the little children to come unto me, and forbid them not" . . .

Somebody said these things, because they are staring me in the face at this moment from the Bible. And whoever said them was *gigantic*. And whoever said them was *living* . . . we cannot find in any contemporary literature any phrases which have a shadow of the beauty, the truth, the individuality, nor the *indestructibility* of those phrases.

And remember, I have only quoted five sentences at random. (From *The Fool Hath Said*)

2. *Would* they have invented the material?

Let's assume for a moment that it was possible for the Gospel writers to invent teaching which they attributed to Jesus. Or that the preachers and story-tellers from whom they got their material could have got away with distortion. Even if they had the opportunity, would they have done so?

A good deal of the teaching in the Gospels is about morality – including honesty. Is it likely – or even possible – that some of the finest teaching about honesty which the world has ever known is itself part of a huge lie?

Besides which, material which the Church leaders might have been tempted to invent is not included. For example, there was a tremendous argument in the Church, at the time when the Gospel material was being preached and written. Should Gentile Christians be made to keep the Jewish law of circumcision? It nearly split the Church in two.

If Jesus had given clear teaching on this, the matter would have been settled easily. But he didn't; so the Gospels do not contain such teaching. An inventor – even a well-meaning one – would almost certainly have included something on this problem. To quote John Robinson again: "There seems to have been a reverence for the remembered speech and acts of Jesus which provided an inbuilt resistance to the temptation to make him merely their mouthpiece or puppet."

I am not suggesting that human memories of the first century were equivalent to modern tape recorders. Nor that the Gospel writers mechanically recorded all they were told about Jesus. Nothing could be further from the truth.

Each of the Evangelists approached events in the life of Jesus in an individual manner. Slightly different accounts of some of the sayings of Jesus show that, sometimes at least, they summarised his words. Compare, for example, Matthew 26:64 and Mark 14:62.

In my view these differences *add* to the authenticity of the Gospels. It is clear that we are not dealing with a carefully contrived plot. We have honest accounts by honest men. And I repeat my conviction that the end result is so unexpected, so majestic and so influential, that invention is out of the question – a view shared by many others.

(*Note*: If you want to read more about these questions, I recommend the books listed in the notes on p. 133. Also *I Believe in the Historical Jesus* by I. Howard Marshall (Hodder 1977)).

3. Do the Gospels ring true today?

The impact of the Gospels on open minds is impressive. The classical scholar E. V. Rieu was asked by Penguin Books to make a new translation of the Gospels. On hearing of the invitation his son is reported to have commented: "It will be very interesting to see what Father makes of the Gospels; it'll be still more interesting to see what the Gospels make of Father."

At the end of his lengthy task, Dr. Rieu wrote: "These documents . . . bear the seal of the Son of Man and God, they are the Magna Carta of the human spirit."

More recently, an actor made a similar discovery. Alec McCowen decided to learn St. Mark's Gospel by heart – as a hobby! He was astonished to find that crowded theatres around the world wanted to see and hear his solo presentation of the Gospel. With few props he simply told the story of Jesus as St. Mark recorded it – a great tribute to the power of Alec McCowen's acting and of St. Mark's writing.

The experience made a deep impression on him. He summed it up like this: "Something absolutely marvellous happened in Galilee 2,000 years ago."

4. Can we check any of the details?

Yes, we can. In two ways: by internal examination and by external comparison.

First, we can examine the text itself. When we do this, we make some remarkable discoveries. Some of these are small but significant. Don Cupitt suggests that two Aramaic words point to Luke's integrity as an historian! (in Ian Wilson's *Jesus: the Evidence*). Certainly, two sentences do the same for St. Mark. In one of these Jesus admits his ignorance; in the second he cries out in anguish: *Why?* (see Mark 13:30–32 and 15:34).

Commenting on these passages C. S. Lewis says: "The evangelists have the first great characteristic of honest witnesses: they mention facts which are, at first sight, damaging to their main contention."

Some discoveries are on a larger scale; they can be made only if we study the entire New Testament. For example, Jesus frequently called himself the "Son of Man". In contrast, this title is referred to Jesus in only three other places in the whole New Testament (Acts 7:56; Rev. 1:13 and 14:14). Also significant is the fact that Jesus' emphasis on the Kingdom of God gives way in the preaching of the early Church to three other themes: Jesus himself, and his death and resurrection.

If the New Testament authors invented these and other changes in emphasis and terminology, they were breath-takingly clever. These men were widely dispersed, and without access to telephones or computers. In my view, they would have found it impossible to invent such a subtle story-line, with just the right balance of agreement and divergence. Impossible – unless we add a further invention: a vast flock of well-trained carrier pigeons!

Second, we can test the text against a knowledge of history and geography gained from other sources. John Robinson pointed out that Luke is detailed and accurate at some points, and "extraordinarily vague" at others. He commented: "It is a tribute to him as a historian that where he does not know he does not invent: he generalises." And he cited A. N. Sherwin-White again. This historian studied the trial of Jesus in the light of his detailed knowledge of Roman Law, and of the social practice of the period. He "gave it high marks".

Our ability to check details is often dependent on archaeological finds. Certainly the science of archaeology continues to throw light upon the whole Bible. But this is an important subject, so we will devote two short chapters to it.

We have been studying historical evidence. Any historical "proof" depends upon two things. First, the facts – the documents, objects, eye-witness accounts, etc. Second, the willingness of the investigator to be open to the conclusions to which the facts point.

No one can take you to the Battle of Hastings. If you refuse to believe unless you see it for yourself, then you will never be convinced about anything in history. Not about 1066, nor that Julius Caesar crossed the Rubicon, nor that Jesus taught in Galilee.

Some people refuse to be convinced no matter how strong the evidence. The Flat Earth Society maintained that pictures taken by astronauts were clever fakes. "The earth is flat," they said. End of argument.

The evidence for Christianity is largely concerned with historical proof. All we Christians ask is that the openness of mind which is necessary and proper for the study of history should not be withdrawn just for that period now called the first century AD or CE (Christian Era).

CONCLUDING QUOTATIONS

St. Luke: the most beautiful book ever written – *Ernest Renan*.

Were we to devote to their comprehension (i.e. the Gospels) a little of the selfless enthusiasm that is now expended on the riddle of our physical surroundings, we should cease to say that Christianity is coming to an end – we might even feel that it had only just begun – *E. V. Rieu, on completing his translation of the Gospels*.

Whatever our view of it (St. Mark's Gospel) may be it remains, for good or ill, the most important document in the history of the world, an unrivalled source of information, a corner stone . . .
    But the doubter is entitled to ask – "Is it true?" I cannot prove it, I can only testify to it . . . Week after week, year after year I have been sitting down in front of this Gospel seeking to penetrate it, to keep my mind open to it . . . I can only say that this exercise has only served to reinforce a conviction that in this Gospel we are in the presence of historical, elemental truth – *Stuart Blanch, when Archbishop of York, in* Living by Faith *(D. L. T.)*

It's really a journey through life. It makes sense of the universe we find ourselves in. The story line is tremendous. I think people forget what a good tale it tells – the story of the Children of Israel is the greatest story ever written anyway; and then (with) the coming of Jesus you have a whole new song being sung. So once you get into it, you find it holds together. But also it's so diverse. It's like having a great compendium of friends. It just is the greatest document of the lot, and once you've read it, your life is never the same – *Popular broadcaster, Brian Redhead, who died in January, 1994.*

The teaching of Jesus stands on an Everest alone. No other teaching has had the same impact and influence in countless lives and diverse cultures. No other teaching has provoked so much change, or stirred so much debate – *Professor Sir Norman Anderson*.

10

What about the South Sea Scrolls?

The previous chapter mentioned archaeology. The next two chapters will look more closely at the significance of some of the many scrolls, tablets, etc. which have been discovered in recent years.

"The greatest manuscript discovery of modern times"

The question which forms the chapter heading was put to me by a student. He had heard someone claim that some scrolls had disproved the Bible, but he couldn't remember their name!

He was, of course, referring to the Dead Sea Scrolls. They were discovered in 1947 in caves at Qumran on the north-western shore of the Dead Sea. The scrolls had been stored there by a strict community of Jews which flourished from about 150 BC to AD 68, i.e. before, during and after Jesus' lifetime.

These scrolls remained in eleven caves for 2,000 years, until they were discovered by three Arab boys who were looking after sheep and goats. One lobbed a stone into a cave, heard a *clonk* and made "the greatest manuscript discovery of modern times" (the description is W. F. Albright's).

A few days later Muhammed edh-Dhib, the youngest of the three, went back to explore and found pots containing leather rolls with writing on. He didn't realise that the scrolls were valuable. Nor did anyone else. For some weeks they remained in a tent. Then some of the scrolls were sold for £24 and £7!

They have become more famous than most archaeological discoveries, partly because some writers have suggested that the scrolls cast doubts upon the origins of the Christian Faith. Three men in particular popularised this view: André Dupont-Sommer (a French scholar), Edmund Wilson (an American literary critic) and John Allegro (a British scholar).

In a talk on BBC radio, John Allegro suggested that there were strong similarities between Jesus and the original leader of the Community at Qumran. This man was called the Teacher of Righteousness, and he lived about 100 years before Jesus. Allegro implied that Jesus was not unique, and that Christianity has its roots in the teaching of this Jewish sect, which was flourishing before Jesus was born.

Do the scrolls discredit Jesus?

These novel views were shared by few other scholars. "Nothing that appears in the scrolls hitherto discovered throws any doubt on the originality of Christianity." This sentence was contained in a letter to *The Times* (21st December, 1965). It was signed by eight leading experts in this field. In a book written some years after his broadcast, John Allegro himself admitted that the scrolls do not disprove Christianity.

Work on the scrolls continues, and two Jewish scholars have recently lent their weight to the *un*sensational viewpoint. In his book *The Dead Sea Scrolls*, Geza Vermes does not suggest that they discredit Christianity. True, he does compare Jesus with the Teacher of Righteousness – but only to make the point that

Jesus was a much warmer and less austere person. "Jesus . . . appears as a much more human person, whose concern was with other human persons and their need to be taught how to live as the children of God."

Yigael Yadin made a similar point. This remarkable Israeli – soldier, politician and archaeologist – spent his last years studying the longest of the Dead Sea Scrolls (thirty feet). In *The Temple Scroll*, published in 1985 shortly after his death, he states his controversial conclusion that the Qumran religion influenced John the Baptist, St. Paul and St. John.

He also acknowledged that there was a considerable gulf between the Essenes (the name of the tight, austere community which wrote and preserved the scrolls at Qumran), and the early Christians. The Dead Sea Scrolls show an exclusive community, with a rigid adherence to rules. The New Testament shows an open community, well able to adapt. St. Paul's notion that "love is the fulfilling of the law" would be quite unacceptable to his law-dominated neighbours. These differences proved crucial. The Qumran Community died out; the Christian community thrived.

It is because of Jesus' flexible attitude to religious laws (e.g. "the Sabbath was made for man") that Yigael Yadin calls him "anti-Essene". The British scholar Alan Millard would support this. In 1985 he wrote: "The differences between the Teacher of Righteousness and Jesus are huge."

If the Dead Sea Scrolls do not discredit Christianity, do they relate to it at all? The answer is "Yes", and I will select four areas.

1. Background information: The Essenes shared a country and a culture with Jesus and his disciples. So the scrolls throw light upon the attitudes, the customs, and the divisions in Palestine during the lifetime of Jesus. In this way they illuminate the background against which many of the events of the New Testament took place.

2. A reliable text: Secondly, they increase our confidence in the reliability of the text of the Bible. At least part of every Old Testament book except one (Esther) has been found in the scrolls. These Scripture passages are in Hebrew – the language in which the Old Testament was originally written. They are much older than any other Hebrew Old Testament texts so far discovered – *about one thousand years older*.

Yet a comparison of those parts of the Bible found in the Dead Sea Scrolls with these other much later copies, shows a striking similarity. There are differences of course – this is inevitable over a period of 1,000 years. But the differences do not affect the sense. The *similarities* far outweigh the differences.

It is clear that over the centuries Jewish communities cherished their Scriptures, and copied them with great care. They did all in their power to keep them pure and unchanged, and they were remarkably successful. Because they are very ancient, the Dead Sea Scrolls provide a yardstick by which we can measure that success. As a result they have *increased* our confidence in the accuracy of the Bible.

Magnus Magnusson, of *Mastermind* fame, is a broadcaster with a special interest in archaeology. He speaks of the "very few minor variations" in the scroll of the Book of Isaiah. He continues: "This underlines the essential integrity of the scribal tradition, that a manuscript could be copied over and over again for a thousand years and still preserve an extremely faithful version of the original."

3. *Facts can kill fashions:* We have seen that the scrolls have increased our confidence in the text of the Old Testament. What about the New Testament?

At one time it was fashionable among some scholars to assert that the Fourth Gospel was written late in the second century. They asserted that its key ideas were at home in Greek, rather than in Jewish, culture. In the absence of detailed information it was easy to speculate about a late date. Many scholars viewed the Fourth Gospel as a profound meditation written by a Christian of the second century. It was brimful of spiritual value, but had little historical value.

This plausible theory was killed by two facts. The first fact was the discovery, in the sands of Egypt, of a papyrus fragment from a copy of St. John's Gospel. This was identified in Manchester in 1934 and dated at around AD 130 – pointing to a first-century date for the original.

The second destructive fact was the discovery of the Dead Sea Scrolls. Those who believed that the Fourth Gospel was a free composition written under strong Greek (i.e. Gentile) influence pointed to contrasts drawn by the author. Contrasts like "darkness and light", "good and evil", "life and death". These are *Greek* ideas, they argued, not Jewish. As Jesus was a Jew, the implication was clear. The Gospel was not "earthed" in his life.

Then the scrolls were discovered. They were written by a tightly organised Jewish community. This community rejected all foreign influence – Roman overlords; Greek ideas; everything not thoroughly Jewish.

The text of the scrolls produced some surprises. For one thing, they abound in contrasts – contrasts like darkness and light; good and evil; life and death! It seems that after all, St. John's Gospel reflects *Jewish* thought forms. Rather than emphasising Greek influence, some scholars began to suggest that St. John's is the most Jewish of all the Gospels! Others suspected an Aramaic "first-draft" – and Aramaic was the first language of Jesus (although he would almost certainly have spoken Greek too).

4. *Beware sensation seekers:* Last week I received a postcard from two students who had cycled the length of Britain – 874 miles – to raise money for the fight against Multiple Sclerosis. The postcard shows a group of naked cyclists arriving at Land's End three years earlier. This group wanted to gain publicity for their cause and judged – rightly – that if you cause a sensation, you become well known.

The same principle applies to religious matters. When a Bible scholar says "I believe in Jesus Christ," no one is interested. When a Bible scholar says "I *don't* believe in Jesus Christ" the newspapers are there like a flash.

Careful study of the Dead Sea Scrolls by a host of scholars has *increased* our confidence in the Bible. Yet the views of those few scholars who have tried to use the scrolls to undermine Christianity are more widely known. The student who spoke about the *South* Sea Scrolls shows this very clearly!

No doubt other sensation-stirrers will pick up pens, or sit at word processors, or gather in TV studios, and influence thousands. Christians and serious enquirers will be wise to save their energies for considering criticisms of the Faith with real substance.

Note: in 1992, yet another book on the Scrolls was launched ("hyped" would be a more accurate word) with a "sensational" tag. Geza Vermes (a Scrolls scholar – *Jewish* not Christian) commented that the book was, in reality, "as explosive as a wet mop"!

CONCLUDING QUOTATIONS

It is my considered conclusion, however, that if one will go through any of the historic statements of Christian faith he will find nothing that has been or can be disproved by the Dead Sea Scrolls – *Professor Millar Burrows (Yale University)*.

If the Isaiah scroll is anything to go by, those who take a high view of the authority of the Bible have nothing to fear, and much to gain, from this research (into the Dead Sea Scrolls). It is a staggering fact that in the course of 1,000 years of copying by hand no errors have crept into the text which in any way affect the Bible teaching – *Alan Millard, Rankin Reader in Hebrew and Ancient Semitic Languages, Liverpool University*.

Note: Alan Millard's fine book *Treasures from Bible Times* is a mine of information about archaeology which relates to the Bible (Lion 1985).

POSTSCRIPT ON SCHOLARS AND SENSATIONS

A backbench MP reminded the House of Commons that the Ark was built by amateurs, and the *Titanic* by professionals. It was an important caution. Beware the expert!

Of course we must listen to scholarly experts, and I have already quoted a fair number. But they are fallible human beings like the rest of us, and they can – and do – make mistakes.

Some scholars are too cautious – unwilling to challenge prevailing academic fashions. Others get their facts wrong or show bad judgment – like the eminent historian who lent his support to the faked "Hitler Diaries". (A few years earlier that same historian attacked the Gospels, and got his facts badly wrong about the dating of the New Testament documents.)

As we have seen, a few scholars love to cause a sensation. Recent books from scholarly pens have suggested the following: that the early Christians were "into" drugs and sex – under cover of the moral teaching of the New Testament; that Jesus took a drug before the crucifixion – gambling that he would come through the ordeal alive; that the geography of the Bible belongs to Arabia not Palestine; that Jesus was invented; that Jesus married and divorced . . .

All this can be very alarming to ordinary Christians who don't know whether a particular sensational viewpoint is widely shared by other experts. Professor James Dunn (himself a scholar!) puts all this into perspective:

> Since Christianity and scholarship share the same passion for truth, Christianity and scholarship are in fact natural allies – common foes of all forms of falsehood, distortion and obscurantism.
>
> So Christianity has nothing to fear from scholarship. Scholars may be a different matter! For individual scholars have their biases and prejudices like every other human being . . . But even so, Christianity need have little fear of such scholars. For scholars have to work from the evidence available to them. And evidence has the happy knack of undermining the overblown or unbalanced edifices built upon it.

So far, so good. The fact remains that scholarly sensations often get wide coverage. *Example*: a few years ago a way-out anti-Christian theory was serialised in the *Sunday Mirror*. The book sold four editions in four months around the world. *First result*: one wealthy scholar. *Second result*: several readers concluded that Christianity is untrue.

Scholarly response: a careful letter of protest from a group of academics of "several Faiths and none". They made it clear that the book was not based on sound evidence. Predictably, the letter was sent to *The Times* – and was not read by most people who buy the *Sunday Mirror*. *Concluding plea:* will sane scholars (i.e. the vast majority) make an effort to communicate with us ordinary folk, please?

One more sensation

James Dunn's comments need to be applied to yet another book based on the Dead Sea Scrolls. In 1992, Barbara Thiering from Sydney University wrote *Jesus and the Riddle of the Dead Sea Scrolls*. She added sensational theory to sensational theory. According to Barbara Thiering, Jesus was a member of the sect living at Qumran. He was married with three children when he divorced his first wife and remarried. He did not die on the cross, but lived on and accompanied St. Paul on his missionary travels. Phew!

As N. T. Wright shows in *Who Was Jesus?* (SPCK 1992), this is based, *not on evidence, but on a highly developed imagination* (and perhaps on a desire for fame and fortune: my comment not his). Wright's paperback is both scholarly and readable and I strongly recommend it. In it, he also examines other recent books on Jesus – by Angus Wilson and Bishop Spong.

TAKE A BREAK (4)

He who laughs last . . .
A new church was to be built and the architect said, "It is my practice when designing churches to ask the minister to include one surprise item, and the congregation to include another." Everyone agreed.

The great day arrived. The first few folk came in, and to their great surprise, found only one pew. To their delight it was right at the back where everyone loves to sit. But no sooner had they sat down than the pew rolled smoothly to the front, and another pew popped up in its place. This was repeated until the church was full.

The minister was delighted at his surprise item, as he had the only church in the world which fills up from the front first.

Enthusiasm carried him away as he preached. Then, exactly fifteen minutes into his sermon, a trap door opened in the pulpit, and he disappeared from sight.

*   *   *

Three more bishop stories (the last three, I promise!)
The bishop had a terrible memory for names. At a conference he met one of his clergy. "How is your wife?" he asked. "I'm afraid she died last year, my Lord," was the quiet response. Two days later he met the same man, but – alas – did not recognise him. "How is your wife?" he asked again. "Still dead, my Lord" came the crisp reply.

*   *   *

A Victorian bishop was met at the railway station by a horse and trap. As the pony trotted towards the church where the Confirmation Service was to be held, it loosed wind – as only horses can. The horseman was very embarrassed. "Oh, I'm terribly sorry, my Lord," he spluttered. "Not at all," replied the bishop, heartily. "If you hadn't been so honest, I'd have thought it was the horse."

*   *   *

The Bishop tapped his microphone and asked, "Can you hear me?" "Yes," replied a voice from the back, "but I'm willing to swap with someone who can't!"

11

More Archaeology and Its Implications

Archaeologists working on Biblical sites are keen to explain the nature of their task. They aren't – directly anyway – in the "proof business"; they are concerned with *knowledge*. That is to say, they go to a site to discover what it "says", rather than to prove or disprove the Bible narrative.

They also point out that archaeology, by its very nature, will never be able to answer all our questions – and that it will raise some problems. The spade, the trowel and the sophisticated back-up technology (e.g., determining dates by comparing radioactive carbon with ordinary carbon) often yield incomplete evidence. This is inevitable because archaeologists depend upon a combination of intelligent detective work and happy accident. Archaeology is silent on many questions because the great mass of ancient buildings, walls, tombs and documents have long since been destroyed by damp, or by fire, wind, rain or thieves.

With these important cautions, we can confidently say that Biblical archaeology does two things: it demonstrates the need for a "robust" faith, and it shows that such faith is based on sound information.

A robust faith

Some critics of the Christian Faith want too much evidence. Unless every question is answered in full, they refuse to believe. Conversely, some Christians are too concerned to dot every i and cross every t. They have a "domino" view of the Faith. They are terrified that if one item of evidence is hit sideways, this will eventually knock down the whole building.

Neither approach is compatible with strong Christian faith. C. S. Lewis once declared that Christianity is not a "filleted" religion. In other words, it comes to us with "bones" in – with loose ends and problems. It is coherent but untidy (like life!). Archaeology illustrates this.

Take Jericho, for example. Under Joshua the Israelites marched round that city seven times, and "the walls came tumbling down" (Josh. 6:20). In the 1930s John Garstang of Liverpool University led a team of excavators to Jericho. They found wall stumps and masses of mud bricks. Once more, archaeology had "proved" the Bible. But in 1952, Kathleen Kenyon and her team reopened the quest. She found that Garstang had been mistaken; the flattened walls were in fact about 1,000 years older than he thought. Then Yigael Yadin entered the debate, and disputed Kathleen Kenyon's interpretation of the evidence.

It would be wrong to infer that Kathleen Kenyon disproved the Bible account. In fact, she found part of a building which – together with items of pottery – show that Jericho was inhabited around the time of Joshua's attack (1250 BC). Time and erosion have destroyed other possible clues. The evidence raises questions for the Biblical account, but it neither proves nor disproves its accuracy. In this, as in many other matters, we have to live with uncertainty. Disappointing but true.

Confirmation of faith

A robust faith does not worry too much about dotting i's and crossing t's. Men and women with this kind of faith can live with uncertainties, because their faith is built on solid foundations. Such a faith accepts the silence of archaeological evidence on some issues, and the puzzles which it poses for others. But the Bible is a vital part of this solid foundation, and such Christians are not indifferent to evidence – archaeological or otherwise.

In the last chapter we saw that the Dead Sea Scrolls have *increased* our confidence in both the Old and New Testaments. So far in this chapter I have sounded a cautionary note. I want now to draw attention to a few of the many other archaeological discoveries – in addition to the scrolls – which confirm our confidence in the Bible.

1. First, an ancient feat to rival the Channel Tunnel! "It was Hezekiah who blocked the upper outlet of the Gihon spring and channelled the water down to the west side of the City of David" (2 Chr. 32:30). We know that this is true because it is possible to walk the length of the tunnel – 534 metres – today. Two groups of workmen started digging at each end, and met in the middle in 701 BC.

2. Until recently, we knew about the Roman governor Pontius Pilate only from the New Testament, and from the writings of Josephus, Philo and Tacitus. In 1961 an Italian archaeological expedition working at Caesarea (about 65 miles from Jerusalem) discovered a stone slab. This was inscribed with three names including those of Pilate and of the Emperor Tiberius.

3. In the Acts of the Apostles we read that Gallio was proconsul of Greece (18:12). An inscription discovered at Delphi records a decision made by Emperor Claudius on a matter referred to him by Gallio. From this, historians deduce that Gallio almost certainly began his term of office in the summer of AD 51. This discovery is important because it provides an accurate reference point for fixing other dates. It is one of a large number of details in Acts which have been shown to be correct.

4. Jesus was brought up in Nazareth in the area of Galilee. We are so familiar with the phrase "Jesus of Nazareth" that it comes as a surprise to find that the town of Nazareth is not mentioned in the Old Testament. Some scholars believed the term "Jesus of Nazareth" to be incorrect, even though it is applied to Jesus in the New Testament. They preferred the term "Nazi*rite*" which *is* found in the Old Testament, and refers to an office, not a place.

Excavations in 1955 demonstrated that a town called Nazareth did, after all, exist in Galilee well before the time of Jesus. Commenting on this, Canon Anthony Harvey writes: "This little episode by no means stands alone. It is symptomatic of the way in which archaeology has tended in recent years to enhance the credibility of the Gospel narratives."

5. In 1968 the bones of a crucified man called Jehohanan were discovered. The nail through his feet was still in place, together with fragments of olive-wood. The bones of his lower leg had been broken. These harrowing details agree entirely with the Gospel accounts of crucifixion.

6. We have already noted that the oldest existing portion of the New Testament is a fragment from St. John's Gospel. This papyrus scrap (containing what we now call John 18: 31–33) was preserved in the dry sands of Egypt for nearly 2,000 years. We also saw that the Dead Sea Scrolls have illuminated the historical background of St. John's account. As this is often regarded as the least historical of the four Gospels, it is worth noting that some of its details have been verified by archaeology.

For example, the *Oxford Bible Atlas* (1984) confirms that two important sites have been located by archaeologists. These are the pools of Bethesda (John 5:2) and Siloam (John 9:7), where Jesus is said to have performed healing miracles.

Professor A. M. Hunter summed up like this: "Thus archaeological discovery has, at point after point, tended to confirm John's topography, even if all problems have not been finally solved."

7. The Temple which Jesus visited, and in which he taught, was destroyed (as he predicted) in AD 70, when the Romans

crushed the Jewish rebellion. Little of it remains, but there are two items worth noting.

First, the massive stones which can now be seen in Jerusalem's famous "Wailing Wall". Some of these survived the Roman attack. They are from the huge platform which supported the Temple, not from the Temple itself. The largest stone block measures 16½ feet by 13 feet.

Second, a notice engraved in limestone, discovered in 1871. This stone slab measures about 2 feet by 3 feet and illuminates various Bible passages. Part of a second, similar notice was found in 1936. Investigation showed that the letters were originally painted red (appropriate, as we shall see!).

In Acts 21 Luke describes a riot which began when Paul was accused of taking a Greek friend into the Temple. No wonder! Here is the inscription on the stone: *No foreigner may pass the barrier and enclosure surrounding the Temple. Anyone who is caught doing so will be himself to blame for his resulting death.*

Paul denied the charge. He knew that Gentiles could go so far – and no further. In his letter to the Ephesians, Paul reminded his readers that Jesus has broken down the wall which once divided Jews and Gentiles. Those who knew about the famous Jerusalem Temple, with its sequence of barriers, would readily understand this teaching.

I am tempted to multiply examples. I want to write about Ahab's palace of ivory; about the clay tablets from Ugarit which illustrate the nature religion of Canaan, against which the Israelites were constantly warned; about the three chariot cities of Solomon; about the amazing engineering feats of Herod the Great (or, more accurately, Herod the horrible); about . . . But I must be disciplined! So I will end with a summary, and then let the experts speak for themselves.

Summary

The list of archaeological discoveries which relate to the Bible is impressive. Difficulties remain, of course. There are still many points where our knowledge about people, places, and dates is incomplete or confused.

In any case, archaeological evidence is *indirect* evidence. It demonstrates that at many points the Bible is historically reliable. It provides information which helps us to understand customs and attitudes in Bible times. But it cannot prove or disprove the truth of Christianity. And it certainly cannot prove or disprove the existence of God.

What it *does* show is that we may approach the Bible with confidence. When we add to this the evidence for the New Testament text outlined earlier, our confidence grows. As the Bible is basic material for the Christian Faith, this is an extremely important first step.

CONCLUDING QUOTATIONS

. . . it is a fact that, by and large, modern archaeological science has done a great deal to confirm the accuracy of the history recorded in the Bible, and only rarely and in relatively unimportant matters does it put a question mark against the biblical record – *Professor I. Howard Marshall.*

. . . it may be stated categorically that no archaeological discovery has ever controverted a biblical reference – *Professor Nelson Glueck – one-time President of the Hebrew Union College Biblical and Archaeological School.*

There can be no doubt that archaeology has confirmed the substantial historicity of the Old Testament tradition – *Professor W. F. Albright.*

Archaeology has indeed corroborated the substantial historicity of the Biblical record from the patriarchal period to the apostolic age, but it is not by archaeology that the essential message of the Bible can be verified. Sometimes. . . indeed, archaeology has made the interpretation of the Biblical narrative more difficult rather than less so – *Professor F. F. Bruce.*

So far, archaeology has really only scratched the surface, metaphorically speaking. But with every month and every year, new archaeological discoveries are lighting up our knowledge and our understanding of the Bible lands BC – *Magnus Magnusson.*

12

Too Violent, Too Old, Too Contradictory

At the end of this section of questions about the Bible, we shall look briefly at three further objections.

A violent book

This cannot be disputed. The ancient world was a violent world. Fighting between nations was universal, and Israel was no exception. Many battles are described in the Bible, and the Israelites prayed for God's help as they fought.

But the Israelites were different from their neighbours in many ways. They knew that certain forms of violence were forbidden – human sacrifice for example. And their teachers and prophets emphasised the importance of offering care and hospitality – especially to orphans, to widows, and to foreigners within their borders.

Two further points are relevant. *First*, the Bible is an honest

book. It refuses to whitewash its heroes. The cowardice of
Peter is not hushed up. But it is not recorded as an example to
be copied. In the same way, the violence of David (2 Sam.
11:14–15), and of the poet who wrote Psalm 137, are there for
all to see. But their violence is condemned by the very
Scriptures which describe so honestly these human failings.

Second, the Bible shows moral and spiritual development. I
am not suggesting that we find a smooth progression from
violence to love. The upward path was very uneven, and some
Old Testament characters were streets ahead of many in the
New Testament, or in the modern world.

But development there is. Slowly, over the centuries, God
taught them more and more about love and forgiveness. The
climax came when Jesus told his astonished hearers: "Love
your enemies." He put his own teaching into practice. On the
cross he prayed for his torturers: "Father, forgive them, for
they do not know what they are doing."

An old book

The Bible is about people whose transport was limited to
horses and camels (or feet) over land, and wind in sails or oars
across water. How can it have anything relevant to say to a
generation which can get to the moon?

If we concentrate on surface differences – clothes, customs,
travel – we shall see ourselves as totally different from the men
and women we read about in the Bible. Logical conclusion?
That the Bible has nothing useful to say to the modern world.

Certainly, we should not underestimate the differences: in
many ways their attitudes and assumptions were *very* different
from ours. Quite often we need to probe hard into that world,
before we can make good sense of the Bible.

But the *similarities* between Bible characters and ourselves
are enormous too. Many of the problems they faced are our
problems: the cost of living, war and peace, getting on with
other people, making sense of life. We find in the Bible people
who fell in love, people who hated, people who were anxious
and afraid, people who worked, people who laughed and cried,
people who became ill, people who grew old, people who died.

The Bible is about men and women like that, and about activities like that. It deals with the "constants" in human life, and it deals with them in a profound way.

It was a book for the first century. It is a book for the twentieth century. It is a book for all ages.

Full of contradiction and error

It will be obvious from earlier chapters that I don't agree with this objection, for I have a high view of the Bible's reliability. I readily agree that we must read the Bible intelligently – accepting the different kinds of writing (history, poetry, parable, law, etc.) for what they are. And I readily accept that any library of sixty-six books written by authors and editors over a thousand-or-so years, is likely to contain many differences of viewpoint and approach. Indeed, it is the overall *unity* of the Bible's message which impresses me, not any apparent errors and contradictions.

But nothing is gained by pretending that problems don't exist.

Some religions protect their holy books from close critical scrutiny. For example, Muslims and Mormons claim that the Qur'ān and the Book of Mormon came directly from God – by dictation and by tablets respectively. In contrast, the full human involvement of the writers of the Bible is freely acknowledged by Christians. We believe that God's Spirit guided those men as they wrote, by using – not bypassing – their personalities, gifts, and experiences. God certainly didn't tidy up Mark's rough Greek style! This is an *encouragement*, not a problem, for it shows that God can use us – warts and all.

However, while I do believe that God inspired and guided the writers, I haven't tried to prove this. I have attempted something more modest – to demonstrate that the Bible (especially the Gospels) is sufficiently accurate, reliable and strikingly original, for us to take it very seriously.

As stated earlier (page 104), my concern is for a robust faith – a faith which can face problems and live with untidiness. This is such an important point that I will close by describing two believers who admitted that they found problems in the Scriptures. They didn't pretend. They didn't despair. They acknowledged the difficulties, but kept them in perspective.

For their faith was, and is, built on solid foundations, which can't be shaken by small details.

John Calvin, the great sixteenth-century Reformer, had a very high view of the Bible, and he wrote long books of exposition. In Matt. 27:9 the Evangelist quotes the Prophet Jeremiah. Calvin knew the Old Testament so well that he recognised this to be an error. He commented: "I confess I do not know how the 'Jeremiah' came in here, and I do not worry much. Certainly it is an obvious mistake to put Jeremiah for Zechariah, for we do not find anything like it in Jeremiah." He then proceeded to write thousands more words of Bible exposition. This small point did not in the least disturb his belief in the Bible as the Word of God.

A modern example comes from the pen of *Professor Howard Marshall* of Aberdeen University. Mark and Matthew give rather different accounts of the healing of Blind Bartimaeus (Mark 10:46–52; Matt. 20:29–34). In Mark there is one blind man; in Matthew there are two. Professor Marshall comments: "It seems probable that Matthew has doubled the numbers without any historical basis in the stories themselves; it is possible that he was trying to indicate that Jesus performed more healings of the same kind than he had space to record as separate incidents."

This does not shake his belief in the overall reliability of the Gospel accounts. This is shown by the title of the book from which I have quoted: *I Believe in the Historical Jesus* (1977). Nor does it disturb his view of the Bible as inspired Scripture. Later, he wrote a book entitled *The Inspiration of the Bible*. He concludes this by movingly describing the basis of his own faith: "It is through the Bible that I know of the God who has declared his salvation in the life, death and resurrection of Jesus, and with deepest thankfulness I embrace that saving truth and stake my life on it."

Note: After writing the note on John Calvin, I looked up Matthew 27:9 in the scholarly *Peake's Commentary*. The writer agrees that the quotation is from Zechariah, but he adds "with certain allusions to Jeremiah 18:2–3 and 36:6–15". So perhaps Matthew wasn't quite as wrong as Calvin supposed!

Part IV

Questions about Suffering

My God, my God, why have you forsaken me?
Psalm 22:1 and Mark 15:34

It was only when I lay there on rotting prison straw that I sensed within myself the first stirring of good. Gradually it was disclosed to me that the line separating Good and Evil passes, not through States, not between classes, not between political parties either – but right through every human heart – and through all human hearts . . . And that is why I turn back to the years of my imprisonment and say, sometimes to the astonishment of those about me: "*Bless you*, prison!"
Alexander Solzhenitsyn

13

Why Does God Allow Suffering?

As I write, the world news is bleak. War in Europe; famine in parts of Africa; an earthquake in Los Angeles. An avalanche in the French Alps has killed six skiers, including five British doctors – with one remarkable escape. A serial killer terrifies parents and children in South Africa. Children are abused, neglected and murdered in Britain.

The grim words of Jesus have again been grimly fulfilled: "For nation will rise against nation, and kingdom against kingdom. There will be famines and earthquakes in various places" (Matt. 24:7).

Life isn't all gloom and doom however. I have just been given a paperback entitled *Chase* in which a policeman describes his narrow escape from death. A bullet hit his teeth, and the tough enamel ("a kind of organic steel") deflected it. He believes that God saved his life.

On a lighter note, a letter in the *Church Times* describes the breakdown of a family car, followed by a child's question: "Why don't we pray about it?" Rather embarrassed, they did. And – you've guessed it – help arrived. Next week, the predictable questions were raised. Why should God answer *that* prayer in that way? Isn't that favouritism? Starving believers pray too; where is God's bounty then?

Well, we have it on the highest authority that God *does* have a preference for childlike prayers. But the questioners have a point too. Surely some of these suffering believers are children. Why, then, is God silent? Why does God allow such terrible things to happen? This is the most difficult question of all, for those who believe in an all-loving and all-powerful God. Is there an answer? Certainly there is no easy answer and anyone addressing this great mystery, in a world of hurting people, must do so in a spirit of deep humility. But still the question persists, and a sense of inadequacy cannot be used as an excuse for saying nothing.

As we consider the problem it becomes clear that the fact of suffering raises, not one, but *two* theological questions – as well as a host of practical questions about effective action.

First question: Why does God allow these things to happen?
Second question: Does God really care for us? Indeed, is he really there at all? We will look at each of these in turn.

1. Why?

Why does God allow such things to happen?

The short answer is that, usually, we simply do not know. When we consider why this particular accident happened, or why that particular child died so young, we are forced to admit that we can give no answer. This becomes especially difficult in the light of claims by other people that God *did* step in and help them.

Sometimes, of course, the reasons for suffering are all too clear. We inflict it on one another. Most starvation in the modern world is caused by corrupt or inefficient government, by unfair trading or by war. Of course, drought and other natural causes play a part. But it is the political context which is so often decisive. It seems that God gives us the freedom to love one another – or to harm one another. Tragically, we often choose the latter course; we live in a "fallen" world.

Jesus himself accepted suffering as an inescapable ingredient of life. He made it clear that we must never assume that personal disaster is God's punishment for personal sin (Luke 13: 1–5). Certainly we must never act as judge in such matters. That is God's work, not ours.

God has created the world with a life of its own – "a world that makes itself". Accidents *happen*, they are not "sent". We live in a beautiful and exciting world, but it is sometimes unpredictable and often dangerous. Some scientists (e.g. Dr. Arthur Peacocke) assert that the act of creation inescapably involves the fact of suffering. You can't have one without the other.

Time and again Jesus repeated the phrase: "Don't be afraid". He wasn't an escapist. He didn't pretend that the sky is always blue. He lived in a cruel and dangerous world which eventually crucified him. But he knew that we are never abandoned by God – even though we may sometimes *feel* abandoned. Even death itself is not the final disaster which we imagine it to be.

But when confronted by tragedy, questions press in on us. Why *this* earthquake? Why did God allow *that* accident? Reluctantly we admit that, usually, we can give no answer.

We need to remember, however, that to say that we do not know the reason is quite different from saying that there is no reason. When my television set went wrong, I had no idea why it gave a thin bright band instead of a picture. But I was quite sure that a reason existed, which is why I sent for a television engineer.

2. Does God care?

Behind the question *Why?* stands this further question. We have an uneasy feeling that the God who allows these things to happen may not really care for us – if he exists at all.

Does God exist? Is he indifferent? Or does God love the world which he has created? Here we can give a clear and definite answer, for we have clear and definite evidence. Yes, God *does* love us. We know this because he has given us a clear demonstration of his love. *He sent his Son to die for us*.

At first, this might seem to be a rather slick answer. In fact, it is the greatest of all answers, to the greatest of all questions. It is the keynote of the New Testament. Does God love us? To this question the Bible replies: "For God so loved the world that he gave his only Son" (John 3:16).

Here, as always, it is the person of Jesus who makes sense of life – and death. The fact of Christ is the answer to the problem of suffering.

This is supported by another kind of evidence – the fact that people often speak of experiencing the strength of God *in and through* their suffering. Bishop Leonard Wilson was taken prisoner during the Second World War. He was tortured, and his tormentors taunted him: You believe in God. Why doesn't he save you? The bishop replied that God did save him – not by removing the pain, but by giving him the strength to bear it.

After the war, he confirmed a man whose face seemed familiar. He realised that the man had been one of his interrogators. The bishop's faith as he suffered had convinced that man of the reality of Christ.

The balance principle

Very often life demands that we "weigh" facts. A friend is accused of theft. There is evidence which appears to be against him. He was outside the supermarket with items in his bag – items which he hadn't paid for.

What can we put on the other side of the balance? We *know* our friend. All our experience of him suggests that he is honest. We know that when he found fifty pounds, he handed it to the police.

The fact that he was found with the goods presents a problem for our faith in our friend. Against this evidence, we balance our personal knowledge of him. Then we decide which way the balance must come down.

Of course, we may suspect that our friend is *dis*honest – in which case there is nothing we can put on the right-hand side. It is not the details which matter here, but the way in which we tackle a problem like this.

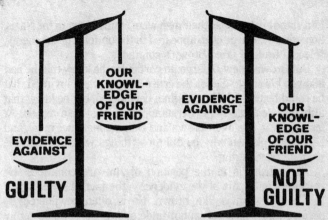

This "balance principle" provides the key to the solution of the problem which pain and suffering present for our belief in God. We must insist on looking at *all* of the evidence. The atheist will draw our attention to part of the evidence – the fact of suffering. We must take this into account. Certainly it weighs heavily on the left of the balance.

But we must also take into account the fact of Jesus Christ, and the not uncommon experience of unexpected strength in suffering. This too is evidence. If it is true that God sent his Son, and that he continues to send his Spirit, because he loves us, then this tips the scale. Two further illustrations will make the issues clearer.

1. *An imaginary war story*: During the last war Mr. Brown was involved with the French Resistance movement. He was introduced to M. Defarge who, he was told, was head of the whole operation. They worked together and Mr. Brown was tremendously impressed with M. Defarge.

On one occasion they planned to blow up an ammunition store. It was almost certain that those who took part would die. Defarge's son volunteered, and with much grief Defarge allowed him to go. The mission was successful but his son was killed.

One day Defarge told Brown that they must alter their tactics. He warned Brown that he would see him doing things which he would not understand. On occasions, Brown saw Defarge helping their own men to escape. At other times Brown saw

him standing by while their men were handed over to the Nazis.
Sometimes Defarge even appeared in the uniform of the enemy.
"He is a traitor!" cried Brown's comrades.

But Brown knew Defarge. In particular, he knew that he had
allowed his son to die for the cause. Brown was convinced that
he could be trusted. He was often bewildered, but he knew that
although he could not understand, there must be a reason. At
last, the war was over. Brown and Defarge met once more, and
Defarge explained why he did those things which at the time
were so bewildering.

The atheist is in the position of Brown's comrades. He
considers only part of the evidence – the fact of suffering.

The Christian is like Brown. He is often bewildered by
occurrences which he cannot understand. His faith is sorely
tried by terrible events which suggest that God does not care.
But he knows God. Above all he knows that God sent his Son to
die for us. It is because of this that he is certain that God loves us.

2. *An incident from the mission field*: This time we are
dealing with fact. John Paton was a Christian missionary. In
1858 he and his young pregnant wife went to the primitive
Island of Tanna in the New Hebrides. During the first year she
died of fever. This was followed seventeen days later by the
death of their one-month-old son. Grief-stricken, John Paton
buried his wife and child. He recorded these words:

> It was very difficult to be resigned, left alone, and in sorrowful
> circumstances; but feeling immovably assured that my God
> and Father was too wise and loving to err in anything that He
> does or permits, I looked up to the Lord for help, and struggled
> on in His work. I do not pretend to see through the mystery of
> such visitations – wherein God calls away the young, the
> promising, and those sorely needed for His service here; but
> this I do know and feel, that, in the light of such dispensations,
> it becomes us all to love and serve our blessed Lord Jesus so
> that we may be ready at His call for death and Eternity.

Notice: "I do not pretend to see through the mystery . . ." To
the question *Why?* he could give no answer. No doubt he

prayed that God – the source of all love and power – would step in to heal. He could not understand why he did not do so. But to our second question – *does God care?* – John Paton affirmed that God is a Father who loves.

This is the authentic voice of faith. *The person with a living faith is often bewildered, but he is prepared to live with questions which he cannot answer, in the light of the great answers which he* does *possess.*

Such faith is not a blind refusal to face the facts. Rather, it comes from a concern to take into account *all* the facts: the fact of suffering *and* the fact of Christ. Such faith is not based on a refusal to consider the evidence. Indeed it springs from a refusal to leave out that part of the evidence which non-Christians so often ignore – the evidence of God's love shown by the fact that he sent his Son and that he continues to strengthen us by his Spirit.

But all this raises another big question. Is the coming of Jesus Christ into our world a fact of sufficient importance to weigh down the scales? Clearly the whole solution depends on this. Is Jesus *that* significant? We shall turn to this question next. But before we do so, two other brief but important points.

1. Suffering and the Cross of Christ

A few years ago I was interested in buying a print based on a Russian icon. Proceeds from the sale would help Christians in Eastern Europe, and I am moved by some Russian art, so it seemed a happy combination. Then I read the description. The picture showed Jesus in Glory. He was strong and serene – apparently above, and untouched by, the sufferings of the world.

I decided not to buy that picture after all. No doubt it conveyed deep truths about the vindication and glorification of Jesus. But it seemed to me to distort the meaning of the Cross.

Jesus is no mere spectator of the anguish of the world. He understands it *from the inside*. He is able to sympathise with our weakness, because he was tempted. He is able to enter into our suffering, because he has suffered. We are required to forgive those who harm us, because he forgives us.

And if this suggests a sympathetic Son of God, and an

indifferent God, let us recall that fathers suffer in the anguish of their children. "God was in Christ reconciling the world to himself" (2 Cor. 5:19, RSV).

2. Suffering and weakness

Some people triumph over pain and tragedy with a glowing and untroubled faith. But it isn't always like that. The apostle Paul wrote to the Church at Corinth "out of much affliction and anguish of heart and with many tears". And the shortest verse in the Bible is amongst the most moving: "Jesus wept" (John 11:35).

It is clear that we are sometimes called to share our *weakness*, rather than our strength.

I recall a friend whose wife died when he was a curate. They had three young children and he attempted to keep the family routine as steady as possible. He went shopping and the tears flowed. He felt an abject failure.

Here was a marvellous opportunity to encourage his parishioners with the strength of his faith – and all he could do was cry! Later he came to see that his tears encouraged them more than his strength would have done. He began to understand what St. Paul meant when he said that God's strength "is made perfect in weakness" (2 Cor. 12:9).

CONCLUDING QUOTATION

On p. 146 we shall consider the death by cancer of Hugh Anderson, aged twenty-one. Reflecting on this tragedy, his father wrote:

> People used continually to ask us why a young man of such promise, and with such a zest for life, should be allowed to die so young. To this the only reply, we both feel, is that we do not, and cannot, know. The vital question to ask God in such cases is not, "Why did you allow this?" (to which he seldom, I think, vouchsafes an answer), but, "What do you want to teach me through this?" – *Professor Sir Norman Anderson in his autobiography*, An Adopted Son.

Part V

Questions about Jesus

I believe there is no one lovelier, deeper, more sympathetic and more perfect than Jesus . . . not only is there no one else like him, but there could never be any one like him.

Fyodor Dostoyevsky

Something absolutely marvellous happened in Galilee 2,000 years ago.

Alec McCowen

The Christ of the Christians is a quite concrete, human, historical person: the Christ of the Christians is no other than *Jesus of Nazareth*.

Hans Küng

14

Was Jesus Invented?

Christ was born about seven years before Christ. This remarkable fact is not due to a major miracle; it is due to a minor miscalculation. The fact that the calculation was made at all *is* a miracle.

The odds against that particular baby becoming so famous must be a trillion, trillion, trillion to one. Nevertheless, it remains true that several hundred years after his death, this village carpenter had become so important that it was decided to date the calendar with reference to his birth. But his birth was so obscure that they got the dates wrong!

Christians rejoice in Jesus' humble origins. And we rejoice that it was *after* his death that he made an impact on the world outside Palestine. We rejoice, for this convinces us of the reality of the resurrection (see Chapter 16).

But these facts present problems too. Roman politicians and

historians were not interested in a young carpenter turned preacher. They began to sit up and take notice only when the dust began to settle in Palestine – and to blow around elsewhere in the Empire. This didn't happen until some years after his execution.

As a result there is a great deal that we *don't* know about Jesus. We don't even know the colour of his eyes, his height and weight, or whether he was good-looking, ugly, or just plain ordinary. Countless artists and film directors have tried to fill *that* particular vacuum!

Because of this time gap, it is possible to speculate as to whether Jesus really existed. Perhaps his followers invented him – though it would be inaccurate to call them "followers" if they had!

During the last two centuries, some scholars have argued for this. In the Soviet Union, children were taught that Jesus was a second-century invention. He was invented, they said, to account for an early Communist movement.

Significantly, few recent historians have gone down that road. So Professor W. D. Davies could say: "The existence of Jesus as a historical figure is not now seriously questioned." Another scholar – C. J. Cadoux – put it even more strongly: "The idea is quite fantastic, and has not been championed, so far as I know, by any competent historian."

But those judgments have been challenged by G. A. Wells, an English professor of German. He argues that Jesus was the product of the imagination of St. Paul and his fellow Christians.

In any case, the idea that Jesus didn't really exist surfaces from time to time in conversations about Christianity, so the need to produce evidence cannot be ducked. This evidence has three separate strands.

A. Evidence from ancient non-Christian sources

Because space is limited and this information is readily available elsewhere (see page 132), I will not attempt to give a full account of the evidence from ancient non-Christian sources. But I will make three points:

1. A taster: To give you a taste of the evidence – and the problems which accompany it – I will set out a famous quotation from the Jewish historian Josephus, who was born about AD 37. He defected to the Romans in the Jewish-Roman war which started in AD 66, and which is referred to in the Gospels. Josephus mentions Jesus in two passages in his famous *Antiquities*. Here is the longer of the two:

> Now, there was about this time Jesus, a wise man, *if it be lawful to call him a man,* for he was a doer of wonderful works, a teacher of such men as receive the truth with pleasure. He drew over to him both many of the Jews, and many of the Gentiles. *He was (the) Christ.* And when Pilate, at the suggestion of the principal men amongst us, had condemned him to the cross, those that loved him at the first did not forsake him; *for he appeared to them alive again at the third day; as the divine prophets had foretold these and ten thousand other wonderful things concerning him.* And the tribe of Christians, so named from him, are not extinct at this day.

I have put some sentences in italics because many scholars believe these to be later Christian insertions. But most scholars believe the rest to be authentic, for there is no textual evidence against either of Josephus' "Jesus passages".

2. The importance of what the Rabbis didn't say. From the Tannaitic period of Jewish history (AD 70–200) we have a few references to Jesus. By this time Jews and Christians were in dispute, and it would have suited Jewish teachers to be able to cast doubt upon the existence of Jesus. They did not do so.

Quite the reverse. In the Jewish Talmud Jesus is acknowledged as a Jew, and described as an executed false teacher. His miracles, teachings and disciples are all referred to. Professor F. F. Bruce sums up: "The rabbis of this period, then, were not unacquainted with the story of Jesus and the activity of his followers, vigorously as they voiced their dissent from all that he and they stood for."

3. There is more evidence for Christians than for Christ. Those
Roman officials and historians who took an interest in the
Christian movement did so reluctantly. For the word Christian
seemed to be spelt T-R-O-U-B-L-E. So Pliny the Younger (Roman
Governor of Bithynia: AD 110–113), Suetonius (a Roman historian who wrote around AD 100), and Tacitus (a Roman historian
born in AD 56) were more interested in the antics – as they
regarded them – of the early Christians than in Jesus himself. But
they did not doubt that behind it all was a man called Christ. For
example, in his *Annals*, Tacitus describes how the Emperor Nero
used the Christians as a scapegoat for the burning of Rome.

> Therefore, to scotch the rumours, Nero substituted as
> culprits, and punished with the utmost of cruelty, a class
> of men, loathed for their vices, whom the crowd styled
> Christians (*Christianos*). Christus, the founder of the name,
> had undergone the death penalty in the reign of Tiberius, by
> sentence of the procurator Pontius Pilate . . .

Of course, Tacitus never met Jesus. He knew about Jesus
from the Christians of his day – and perhaps from another
important source too. As Professor Bruce points out, Tacitus
enjoyed high status, and might have had access to official
Roman records.

To sum up: I readily acknowledge that we do not have vast
quantities of detailed information about Jesus from these early
non-Christian sources. In the nature of the case we would not
expect this. It was only when the Christian movement would
not lie down – despite slander, scorn and persecution – that
politicians and historians began to take notice.

Indeed, I would argue that the lack of detailed information,
far from being a problem, *lends weight* to the Christian case.
How on earth did Jesus become so famous, some time *after* his
life and death in relative obscurity? This *fact* points clearly to
his resurrection. But we shall devote an entire chapter to this.

On the basis of the evidence we do have, we can be quite
sure of two things. *First*, that Jesus existed. *Second*, that he was
a notable teacher, that he gained a reputation as a miracle
worker, that he offended authority, and that he was executed.

The evidence for these points from non-Christian sources is supported by two other sets of data.

B. Early Christian evidence

In addition to the inevitably sparse comments from Roman and Jewish sources we have a large quantity of early Christian material. In particular, we have the Gospels. I shall not repeat my reasons for believing them to give a substantially accurate account of the life of Jesus (see Chapters 9–12). But I will make three points.

First: many of the finest, most detailed studies of great people have come from their friends or followers – for example, Boswell on Johnson and Plato on Socrates. Of course, we make allowances for bias. But we also recognise that close friends are the only people who have detailed, accurate information.

Second: the Gospels were a totally new and unique form of literature. *Something happened* in first-century Palestine which produced an unparalleled burst of joyful, creative energy. Everything about the Gospels suggests that they were *inspired by someone* (or Someone), not cooked up by clever inventors.

Professor C. S. Lewis immersed himself in literature of all kinds. Writing about St. John's Gospel he gave this judgment:

> Either this is reportage – though it may no doubt contain errors – pretty close up to the facts ... Or else, some unknown writer in the second century, without known predecessors or successors, suddenly anticipated the whole technique of modern, novelistic, realistic narrative. If it is untrue, it must be narrative of that kind. The reader who doesn't see this has simply not learned to read.

Lewis makes it clear that the first possibility has all of his votes.

Third: if the men who produced the Gospels were inventors, they were incredibly subtle – building in a complicated range of difficulties – or very hamfisted as historians. Brilliant inventors would have included a few problems, of course – but they would not have risked so many loose ends and unresolved questions. Some of those notorious differences between the Gospels would certainly have been ironed out! The fact they did not do a tidier job strongly suggests that the Gospel writers were faithful to their sources and to their memories.

Don Cupitt and Peter Armstrong make this point in *Who Was Jesus?*

> If the Gospels are myth dressed up as historical fact, then the job has not been done very well . . . If a myth is being projected back into history, why this bit of history, and why create needless difficulties?

C. Modern witnesses

This brings me to the third and final strand in the evidence for the reality of the historical Jesus. He is "solid" enough to make a tremendous impression upon a wide range of people in our century. Here are a few examples.

A Communist. In the 1970s a Czech, Milan Machovec, wrote *A Marxist Looks at Jesus*. He acknowledged that Jesus "set the world on fire", and he explains why: ". . . he himself was the attraction. They saw in him a man who already belonged to this coming Kingdom of God; they saw what it meant to be 'full of grace' . . ."

Two Jewish scholars. Geza Vermes is a Jewish scholar based in Oxford. He warmly acknowledges Jesus as a fellow Jew who was "an unsurpassed master of the art of laying bare the inmost core of spiritual truth".

Martin Buber, a great Jewish leader of our century, goes as far as a Jew can, without actually becoming a Christian! "From my youth onwards I have found in Jesus my great brother . . . I am more than ever certain that a great place belongs to him in Israel's history of faith and that this place cannot be described by any of the usual categories."

A famous Hindu. It is said that Mahatma Gandhi had a crucifix in his office, and that "When I Survey the Wondrous Cross" was his favourite hymn. Of Jesus he said: "I believe that he belongs not only to Christianity but to the entire world, to all races and people."

Two scholarly sceptics. Don Cupitt is a dean who delights in doubt. He encourages scepticism, and loves to stir a theological scandal. In *Who Was Jesus?* (written with Peter Armstrong) he warns us not to accept the Gospels as a simple, straightforward record. Despite this he speaks highly of St. Luke's integrity as a historian. And he does not doubt the existence of the historical Jesus:

> We can't promise too much . . . But we suggest that the main themes of his life and teaching can be recovered. Enough does emerge to give us plenty to think about . . . So there is every reason to think that Jesus did in fact exist, and that the world of the Gospels did in fact exist. No one in antiquity suggested he was mythical.

Ian Wilson ends his paperback edition of *Jesus: the Evidence* with a personal statement of belief. He acknowledges that he is a natural doubter and that he finds faith difficult. Then he sums up his position:

> With every sceptical faculty alive and kicking I *do* believe that nearly two thousand years ago, in the land we today call Israel, the "word" . . . *was* made flesh and dwelt in a Galilean Jew called Jesus . . . for a brief moment in history there was magic in the air. The sick were healed, men and women caught a glimpse of heaven, all too good of course to last.

A famous author, H. G. Wells was not a Christian. Nor was he a natural ally of the Christian Church. But his admiration for Jesus was boundless. In his famous *Outline of History* he wrote several fine pages on the impact of Jesus. I will select four sentences:

> He was too great for his disciples . . . He was like some terrible moral huntsman digging mankind out of the snug burrows in which they had lived hitherto . . . Is it any wonder that men were dazzled and blinded and cried out

against him? . . . Is it any wonder that to this day this Galilean is too much for our small hearts?

The point that I am making is simple, but important. The *solidity* and *reality* of Jesus forcibly strikes each of these writers. None of them is biased in favour of Christianity. They are honest witnesses, who acknowledge that Jesus has made a tremendous impact upon them. They find him *convincing, real and "solid"* – a man with three (or four!) dimensions, not two.

He is also unique. Modern novelists often invent "solid" figures. But when they attempt to invent unique, towering figures they come up with someone like Superman. Great fun, but firmly and obviously in the world of fantasy.

On the "invention" theory we are required to believe in the unparalleled creative powers of a group of writers from the early years of the Christian era. They were prepared to suffer and die for their invention. Their achievement was so enormous that they were able to change the world. Calendars were based on their invention. Their skill was so great that their invention is able to convince modern thinkers as discerning and diverse as our witnesses.

It seems altogether more likely that they were inspired and challenged by a Real Person.

Certainly that is how it strikes me. I, at least, am persuaded that we find in the Gospels an uncontrived story, which tells the truth. To invent Jesus would require someone of the stature of Jesus. To invent the subtle differences of emphasis within the Gospels, and to relate them so subtly to the rest of the New Testament, would require a whole collective of geniuses. And genius notoriously comes in ones and twos.

Note: The quotations from Josephus and Tacitus in this chapter are taken from *Invitation to the New Testament* by W. D. Davies (D.L.T. 1967). For a full account of the evidence for Jesus from ancient non-Christian sources, I recommend *Jesus and Christian Origins Outside the New Testament* by F. F. Bruce (Hodder, Second Edition, 1984).

Note: Two fine books have been published with the title *The Evidence for Jesus*. The first (SCM 1985) was by James Dunn, Professor at Durham University (see page 100 for a quotation from his book). The second (Hodder 1986) is by R. T. France, Principal of Wycliffe Hall, Oxford. I also strongly recommend a more recent book by N. T. Wright, *Who was Jesus?* (SPCK, 1992).

CONCLUDING QUOTATIONS

In 1913, the Cambridge mathematician G. H. Hardy "discovered" a brilliant Indian mathematician called Srinivasa Ramanujan. It happened like this . . .

Ramanujan – an Indian clerk with little formal education – wrote a long letter to Hardy which was full of complicated mathematical formulae. This posed a puzzle for Hardy: was the letter a hoax, or was it genuine? Hardy soon realised that even his cleverest student could not have invented the letter; the mathematics were far too advanced and original. He was reading a letter from a mathematical genius.

Hardy remarked: "I had never seen anything in the least like them before. A single look at them is enough to show that they could only be written down by a mathematician of the highest class . . . they must be true because, if they were not true, no-one would have the imagination to invent them".

It seems to me that the same can be said of much of the material in the New Testament – and especially those claims made for and by Jesus. *They simply must be true, because no one would have had the imagination to invent them* – least of all *Jewish* men and women to whom they would have been so shocking. You would need someone of the stature of Jesus to invent the extraordinary story of Jesus.

TAKE A BREAK (5)

Many a true word . . .

Two ministers who often disagreed met at a Unity Service. "Still about the Lord's business, Geoffrey?" asked Philip. "Yes," replied Geoffrey, "I'm sure we are *both* about the Lord's business. You in your way, and me in His."

. . . spoken in jest

A young inexperienced Anglican curate was working in a Canadian city. The bishop summoned him. "I've got a job for you, out in the country." The curate was nervous. He would be on his own, and hundreds of miles from home. What would happen if he met a situation he couldn't cope with? "Don't worry," replied the bishop. "If you get any problems, just phone me."

Everything went very well and the curate was warmly welcomed by the people in the villages. Sadly, one day an elderly man died. The family invited the curate to conduct the funeral, but on enquiring further, he discovered that the man was a life-long Methodist. "I'd love to conduct the service," said the nervous curate, "but first I must check with the bishop."

"Bishop," asked the curate on the phone, "a Methodist has died, may I bury him?"

"Go ahead, son," responded the bishop enthusiastically. "Bury as many Methodists as you can."

(Note: my warm thanks to two Methodist friends who read the manuscript, and allowed this story to stay in!)

*   *   *

A clergyman friend of mine says that he can always travel in comfort – even in the rush hour. The trick is simple. He travels by train, wears his dog-collar, leans out of the window at every stop, and beckons to people to join him. It would probably work even without the dog-collar. Try it some time!

15

Jesus, Buddha, Muhammad – What's the Difference?

What was Jesus *really* like?

Christianity is based, not only on ideas, but on events. At its centre we do not find a theory, but a person – the person of Jesus Christ.

He is a person who is widely misunderstood. Many people have a false, sentimental picture. To them Jesus is a rather anaemic character, more interested in flowers, birds and children than in the harsh world of adult reality.

How different is the towering figure of the New Testament! We see there a man marked out as a dangerous rebel by the authorities; a man who drew tremendous crowds; a man who inspired others to deeds of heroism; a man who took the uncompromising road to martyrdom; a man of deep passions and decisive action.

Jesus was interested in children and in nature, of course. And with the down-trodden, he was very gentle. But he was also a man among men. The world he moved in was largely a "man's world" – a harsh world of hatred, intrigue, brutality and revenge. The Gospels portray a dynamic figure who waged war against evil with the weapons of love, openness, kindness and forgiveness. Against those greatest sins of pride, hypocrisy, indifference and humbug his attack was blistering and devastating.

People fitting the above description are rare. But not unique. Other men have shown at least some of these qualities. And a few have been dynamic enough to found great religious movements – Gautama the Buddha who founded Buddhism, and Muhammad the founder of the Muslim religion, for example.

Why should we follow Christ and Christianity, rather than the Buddha and Buddhism, or Muhammad and Islam? These too were great men. Is there any real difference between them?

Are comparisons odious?

I am aware that some readers will not like the question I have just posed. In recent times the term "Comparative Religion" has given way to the "Study of World Religions". The concern is to allow people from different faiths to speak for themselves, in their own terms, without constantly making comparisons.

This shift in emphasis is one with which I have considerable sympathy. For some years I lived in a multi-cultural terraced street. We enjoyed having Muslim and Bahai neighbours, and I am convinced that Christians must listen carefully to members of other faiths.

Certainly we should not attempt to score cheap points. And we must seek to present other faiths in the best possible light. *Every* faith has its share of committed, impressive members. *Every* religion – including Christianity – has its share of horror stories. "Let him who is without sin among you be the first to throw a stone . . ." (John 8:7, RSV).

The fact remains that comparisons made in a spirit of honest enquiry are sometimes inevitable. If one religion claims that a central part of its teaching is unique, that claim can only be tested by comparing it with other faiths. It is in this spirit that I now draw attention to certain aspects of Jesus' teaching.

Was his teaching original?

The answer is an infuriating Yes *and* No! *No*, because Jesus used the Jewish Scriptures as the basis for this teaching. *Yes*, because he constantly brought fresh insights, and made new connections.

For example, his code – love God with all your heart, and your neighbour as yourself – links together two separate Old Testament texts. As for the "Kingdom of God", this notion is certainly found in the Jewish Scriptures. But Jesus put it at *the centre* of his teaching, and illustrated its meaning with a series of brilliant pictures and parables.

One of the clearest examples of the uniqueness of his teaching is seen in a single word. In prayer, his fellow Jews sometimes addressed God as Father. The word they used was rather formal – as when a Victorian son called his father "sir". Jesus used a different Aramaic word: *Abba*. It was a common word in the home. It was very *un*common in prayers, for it was a child's word. "Dad" or "Daddy" is the nearest we can get.

By using that word, Jesus emphasised his own close relationship with God. By encouraging his disciples to use the same word, he emphasised that our discipleship does not have its centre in a set of rules, or even in a way of life. At its centre is a living relationship with the living God, who is *Abba*, Father.

But a loving father is not a doting uncle. The latter can make occasional visits, and indulge his nephews and nieces. A father shares his life and his standards with his children. A father's love includes discipline as well as encouragement. Hence Jesus taught us to love God, to trust God, to obey God – and to "fear" God: to hold him in awe and great respect, for God *is* GOD. He emphasised that forgiveness, prayer, honesty, humility and generosity are all involved in accepting God's kingly rule in our lives.

The authority of Jesus

". . . the crowds were amazed at his teaching, because he taught as one who had authority" (Matt. 7:28,29). No doubt this striking authority had its roots in his powerful personality. But it was emphasised by the content of his teaching. A few examples will illustrate this.

1. The Sermon on the Mount: At the beginning of these three famous chapters (Matt. 5–7) we find the beatitudes. "Blessed are the poor in spirit . . . Blessed are the meek . . . Blessed are the merciful . . . Blessed are the peace makers . . ." They outline the secret of happiness – which is what "blessed" means. Jesus ends these crisp, poetic utterances with the assurance that his followers will be truly happy when they suffer "*for my sake*". When this happens they can rejoice, for their reward in heaven will be great.

In the middle of the sermon, Jesus repeats a telling phrase six times: "You have heard that it was said . . . but *I* tell you" (with stress on the "I").

The sermon ends with a vivid picture of two men: one wise, the other foolish. What is the difference between them? The wise man "hears these words of mine and puts them into practice".

2. Judgment: In various passages, such as the Parable of the Sheep and the Goats (Matt. 25:31–46), Jesus spoke about our final destiny. He calmly assumed that it was he, Jesus, who would judge the world at the end of time.

When we recall that those to whom he was speaking acknowledged only *God* as supreme Judge, we see just how far-reaching this claim was. It is not surprising that the Jewish leaders were determined to kill Jesus, because he was "making himself equal with God" (John 5:18).

3. Worship: When the disciples worshipped him (Matt. 14:33), and when Thomas called him "My Lord and my God!" (John 20:28), Jesus accepted their worship. The tremendous difference between his attitude and that of the Apostles can be seen from Acts 14:8–18. Paul and Barnabas were horrified when the people at Lystra tried to worship them. They knew that only God is to be worshipped, and that for human beings to accept worship is wicked arrogance and blasphemy.

4. *The Last Supper*: In three Gospel accounts of the Last Supper, Jesus institutes a new covenant, "in my blood". The Bible is a book of the Covenant. It describes an "agreement" between unequals: God and his people. Six hundred years before Jesus sat down to eat with his disciples, the Prophet Jeremiah had promised that God would make a new, more glorious, covenant. By his words and actions, Jesus indicated that the great day had arrived at last – and that he, Jesus, was the central figure.

5. *The Temple and the Sabbath*: These were two foundation stones of Jewish society. Jesus challenged both. It was Jesus' dramatic action in overturning the Temple tables that led to his crucifixion, according to the leading American scholar E. P. Saunders. Jesus actually claimed to be greater than the Temple (Matt. 12:6) *and* some great Old Testament characters (Matt. 12:41–42). And in a beautiful passage (about humility!) Jesus asserts that he alone knows God, and that he alone can reveal God (Matt. 11: 25–29).

Let's catch breath at this point. What does this teaching amount to? Note two points: *first*, it is sometimes argued that some of the great claims which Jesus made were read back into his ministry by the early Christians. Possibly: but even if they heightened the effect, *they did not invent them* – for one clear reason. They were God-fearing Jews: strict monotheists. Every day they recited the Shema: "Hear, O Israel: THE LORD our God is one LORD" (Deut. 6: 4, RSV). Notice: *one* LORD.

Given their cast of mind, it would have been impossible for the first Christians to invent the teaching of Jesus. It was forced upon them by things that *actually happened* and words which they *actually heard*.

We can fully sympathise with those Jews who accused Jesus of blasphemy. All that they had been taught demanded it. The idea of exalting a man – however great – to the position which Jesus came to occupy in the disciples' minds was unthinkable: dreadful. *Unless* the evidence for doing so – *evidence presented by the Person himself* – was overwhelming.

Second, Jesus did not go around saying, "I am God." Indeed, he joyfully acknowledged his dependence upon God. He was no usurper. But he did claim a unique relationship with God; he did claim a unique mission from God; and he did claim that he, and only he, could do – and was doing – things which it was proper only for God to do.

This is put very clearly by John Robinson in *Can We Trust the New Testament?* "He steps in the eyes of his contemporaries into the space reserved for God . . . It is impossible to escape the conclusion that he went around not just talking *about* God (that would not have provoked the reaction he did) but standing in God's place, acting and speaking for him."

The alternatives are beginning to emerge. They are stark alternatives. Either this teaching is true; or it is monstrously false. Either Jesus was blaspheming, or he was (and is) the most significant person in all history – the one person of whom it would not be offensive to write Person.

Before developing this point it is worth pausing to consider why it is that this teaching *about* Jesus *by* Jesus is so easily missed – even though it is so widespread in the Gospels. People are often surprised when it is pointed out to them, even when they know the Gospels fairly well.

No doubt one reason is that Jesus' teaching about himself is usually found in the course of his other teaching. He underlines his teaching – about the Kingdom of God, or about forgiveness, or anxiety, or prayer – by reminding his hearers that he has a unique authority to speak on these matters. It seems so natural that we miss its force.

Great men don't need to boast, but they don't need to adopt an attitude of pretend humility either. If Pete Sampras says, "I'm playing good tennis," he is not being conceited. He is simply speaking the truth, and, in the light of this, assessing his chances of winning at Wimbledon.

In the same way, Jesus, with no trace of conceit, says, "All things have been committed to me by my Father," and "Come to me, all you who are weary and burdened, and I will give you rest" (Matt. 11:27 and 28).

But I suspect that the main reason why this teaching is so often overlooked is that it is the very last thing we expect to find. We know that Jesus taught humility. He associated with, and served, ordinary people. He chose working men for his close companions. He lived a simple rough life, and he was prepared to befriend social outcasts.

To find such a humble man saying the sort of things which Jesus claimed for himself is puzzling – even shocking.

It is important to realise that Jesus, alone among the founders of the great religions of the world, spoke in this way. Muhammad and the Buddha claimed to be messengers of the Truth. Muhammad was the "Prophet of God". Gautama became "the Enlightened One" (which is what the word "Buddha" means). They believed that they had a deep insight into Truth; it was this that they wished to pass on.

Jesus claimed to be the very *source and focus of Truth*. There is a chasm of difference between these two attitudes.

Followers of other religions are just as anxious to make this clear as Christians are. The English Buddhist, Maurice Walsh, pointed out that the Buddhist view of Buddha is very different from the Christian view of Christ. He stressed that the Buddha is thought of as a Teacher – *not* as a Saviour.

The same approach applies within Islam. Dr. Geoffrey Parrinder made the point that Muslims "do not like the title Muhammadan", because "they do not worship Muhammad but they believe that he was the last and greatest Apostle of God". How different is Christianity! Christians glory that their name identifies them with Christ, whom they reverence as Teacher, Saviour and God.

Of course, it is impossible not to oversimplify in a mere paragraph or two, and I readily acknowledge the rich complexity of other faiths. But these other towering figures "fit" well within their cultures. Jesus doesn't fit at all well within the culture of Judaism – unless (as he claimed) he fulfils and transcends it.

Was Jesus right?

And so to the really big question. It is one thing to say the things which Jesus said. But were they true?

Notice that I have said that none of the other founders of the great religions of the world have thought of themselves as Jesus did. But I have not said that *no* other men have thought in this way.

Some rulers have claimed to be divine. Herod Agrippa I, for example (see Acts 12:19–24 for details), and some of the Roman emperors. Such rulers were usually proud, arrogant men. Even so, their claims were less far-reaching than those of Jesus. They lived in societies which believed in several gods, so it was just possible for a king to get away with such claims. Jesus and his fellow countrymen believed in *One* God. In their view, claims like those made by the emperors meant only one thing: blasphemy.

Even in modern times we occasionally find people who hold similar views about themselves. In *Basic Christianity*, John Stott recalls a letter which he received. It contained this sentence: "I have just made a great discovery. Almighty God had two sons. Jesus Christ was the first; I am the second." Sadly and predictably, the letter came from a psychiatric hospital.

It is as simple as that. Only three kinds of men could make such claims. An extremely unbalanced person who has great but false ideas about his own greatness; a liar who wants to impress people; or the one Person of whom those claims are true.

There is no fourth possibility. We cannot deny that Jesus' view of himself and his mission is correct, and in the next breath speak of him as a good man and a great teacher. If we refuse to accept his own estimate of himself, the alternatives are much harder than this.

He would not be a good man if he made these claims knowing them to be false. And he would not be a great teacher if he was wrong on this fundamental aspect of his teaching – even if he sincerely believed what he was saying. Either we accept that Jesus was the Son of God, or we number him with the world's lunatics or liars. Sane and moral men – however great they might be – do not speak about themselves as Jesus spoke.

The question which confronts us from the Gospels is clear. Was Jesus insane – falsely believing himself to be divine? Was he a blasphemous impostor – merely pretending to be God's unique Son? Or was he really the Person implied by his majestic claims?

For all Buddhism's rich complexity, we can make sense of the Buddha. In essence, his message is this: "In order to achieve liberation from the ills of this world you need to tread the Path he trod" (Prof. Ninian Smart). It is not difficult to make sense of Muhammad – he was "the Seal of the Prophets" and a dynamic leader. We can easily make sense of Confucius – he was a very wise teacher. We cannot make sense of Jesus at all – unless he really is the Messiah. Or mad. Or bad.

The solution

The only way to decide this question is to examine his behaviour. Does Jesus' character measure up to his claims, or was this just big talk?

Those who lived at the time of Jesus watched him closely. Several of them concluded that his incredible claims were in fact true. They were forced to this decision by the sheer quality of his life – by the combination of sanity, wisdom, humility of life, strength, and transparent goodness.

Some of these were members of a party which opposed Jesus, and they had a lot to lose – leading Jews like Nicodemus and Joseph of Arimathea, for example. And it probably wasn't too good for the military career of the Roman centurion who supervised Jesus' execution as a criminal, to declare: "Surely this man was the (or 'a') Son of God" (Mark 15:39).

Others knew him so well and for so long, that they would have seen through a lie or a bluff. After three years of very close acquaintance with Jesus, Peter could write, "He committed no sin" (1 Pet. 2:22). We find this same thought in John's first letter: "In him is no sin" (1 John 3:5).

We too can examine his character, by reading the Gospels (St. Mark's is probably the best starting point). The issues are far too important to ignore or to shelve. If Jesus really is the Messiah; if he really is divine; if we really are a "visited planet" . . .

If . . .

If these things are true they stagger the imagination. And the practical implications are enormous.

If they are true, we are bound to revise our outlook on life in the light of what he did. We are bound to reorganise our priorities in life in the light of what he said. We are bound to give to this Jesus our obedience and worship. *If* they are true.

If we catch just a glimpse of his significance, we shall – like the wise man in the parable – build our lives on *this* Rock, and none other.

ARCHBISHOP'S POSTSCRIPT

The kind of argument which I have just developed – to point to Jesus as *the* Son of God from whom our sonship (and daughtership!) derives – is sometimes criticised on two counts. *First*, on the grounds that Jesus didn't go round saying "I am God." I readily agree. His immense claims are much more subtle than this. *Second*, because it leans too heavily on the teaching of Jesus as recorded in the Fourth Gospel.

The teaching *about* Jesus *by* Jesus is seen at its clearest there – especially in the numerous "I am" sayings (I am . . . the bread of life; the light of life; the resurrection and the life; the way, the truth and the life, etc.). But many scholars would argue that this is *John's* way of communicating the significance of Jesus. In which case, these are not the actual words of Jesus himself.

In fact, even if it is true, this criticism does not torpedo the argument. For if we ignore St. John's Gospel for this purpose, the staggering claims of Jesus remain.

This is demonstrated very clearly in a fine book by Michael Ramsey. During a distinguished career, he was Professor of

Theology at Durham University, then Archbishop of York and Canterbury. In his paperback *Introducing the Christian Faith* (now sadly out of print) he outlined several of the claims which Jesus made for himself and for his mission. He drew on the first three Gospels only, and he concluded his argument by saying:

> Consider, consider, what claims these are. Are these claims of Jesus true? If they are not true, then the making of them involves either fraud on his part or a terrible self-deception. Perhaps you are trying the line that you welcome Christ's moral teaching and admire it: but reject his own claims. It seems to me a most unconvincing line. The moral teaching and the claims are woven in one, for both concern the reign of God. I see no escape from the dilemma: either Jesus is fraudulent, or his claim is true: either we judge him for being terribly amiss, or we let him judge us. That was, in fact, the dilemma that cut through the consciences of his contemporaries.

CONCLUDING QUOTATIONS

The historical difficulty of giving for the life, sayings and influence of Jesus any explanation that is not harder than the Christian explanation, is very great – *C. S. Lewis*.

No mortal man makes such a claim, or we know him to be mad. We are driven back on the words of wise old "Rabbi" Duncan: "Christ either deceived mankind by conscious fraud, or He was Himself deluded, or He was divine. There is no getting out of this trilemma."

Christians have never been in any doubt which of these propositions is true – *Professor A. M. Hunter*.

We fall too easily into the error of underestimating the originality of Jesus. Even when he used ordinary and familiar words, he poured into them a wealth of new meaning – *Bishop Stephen Neill*.

His words carried divine authority and his actions were instinct with divine power – *Professor C. H. Dodd*.

16

Dead Men Don't Rise

A story is told about Talleyrand, a leading statesman during the French Revolution. He was approached by a dejected friend, seeking advice. His friend had attempted to found a new religion. It was, he said, a considerable improvement on Christianity, but his best efforts had met with little success. What should he do?

Talleyrand paused. He agreed that the difficulties were formidable – so great that he hardly knew what to advise. "Still," he mused, "there is one plan which you might at least try. Why don't you get yourself crucified, and then rise again on the third day?"

Professor Sir Norman Anderson is a distinguished lawyer. He is also a Christian, and he has made a special study of the evidence for the resurrection. His faith has been sorely tested. He and his wife Pat have lived to see their three adult children die.

Their son, Hugh, was a brilliant student at Cambridge when he died of cancer at the age of 21. A few days later, Professor Anderson gave the *Thought for the Day* talk on Radio 4. After explaining why he is convinced that God raised Jesus from the dead, he continued: "On this I am prepared to stake my life. In this faith my son died, after saying 'I'm drawing near my Lord.' I am convinced that he was not mistaken."

They both understood the vital implications of Jesus' resurrection. In the New Testament it is described as the "first fruits" of a great harvest. If Jesus really *did* defeat death, then Hugh's life was not at an end. Indeed, he was making a new and glorious start.

If . . .

In this chapter we shall examine some of the evidence which convinced those two highly intelligent men. But before we do so – two preliminary comments.

1. Christianity stands or falls with this

Resurrection is not simply one aspect of Christianity. We cannot remove a portion of the Christian jigsaw labelled "resurrection", and leave anything which is recognisable as the Christian Faith: we destroy the entire picture. For Jesus himself, his cross, and his resurrection from the dead, are the three foundation stones on which Christianity rests.

People sometimes say: "I'm not bothered about questions like: did Jesus rise from the dead? We've got his marvellous teaching. Surely that's what *really* counts." This "let's-concentrate-on-his-teaching" approach is attractive. But it misses the point. For *without the resurrection it is extremely unlikely that we would have his teaching – or anything else in the New Testament.*

In the early Church there was no preaching of Jesus *except as Risen Lord.* Nor could there be. For without the Apostles' conviction that they had seen Jesus alive again after his death, there would have been no preaching at all.

There would have been deep mourning for a lost friend. There would have been great admiration for a dead hero. No doubt his profound teaching would have been remembered and cherished by his small, loyal circle of followers. But within four generations he would have been forgotten.

Of course, movements do grow and develop after the founder's death – we have ample evidence of this. It happens if the founder's followers are in a buoyant frame of mind – for everything depends on their "get-up-and-go". After Jesus' death, his disciples had just about enough get-up-and-go to restart their fishing business!

Without his resurrection, at the name of Jesus every knee would not bow. More likely, people would say: Jesus who? For many men would bear that name – as they did before he came. In fact, those Jews who acknowledged Jesus to be the Messiah, *and* those who denied him, were reluctant to give this once-common name to their sons – for equal and opposite reasons.

For one group, the name was too high. For the other, it was too low. *Both* opinions point to the tremendous impact made by Jesus – which is another way of saying that they point to his resurrection. It is an interesting commentary on the power of his name, which means "God Saves". Archbishop Michael Ramsey summed it up: "No resurrection; no Christianity."

2. Assessing the evidence is like detective work

No one claims to have witnessed the resurrection. There were people on the spot soon afterwards, but nobody claimed that they saw God raise him up. Sorting out what happened is rather like investigating a murder. But in reverse.

A body is found. No one saw the murder take place, but certain other related facts come to light. Jones was jealous of the victim; a bloodstained axe was found nearby; White's fingerprints were on the wallet ... Detectives, and then lawyers and a jury, try to discover the most likely explanation for these facts. The case is decided if the explanation for each of the facts, or clues, points in the same direction.

It is the same with the resurrection of Jesus, except that the problem is reversed. We are dealing, not with someone said to be murdered, but with someone said to have come alive from the dead. No one saw what happened to the body. But certain other related facts came to light – facts which demand an explanation just as much as the axe and the fingerprints in the murder case.

We shall examine eleven such facts, and try to find the most likely explanation for each of them.

First fact: Jesus died as a young man

Only a handful of men have founded great movements, and made a really decisive impact on history. Each of them needed time in which to make his influence felt. Each of them – except Jesus. For example:

Confucius (The great Chinese teacher)
    Died in 479 BC, aged 72
Gautama the Buddha (Founder of Buddhism)
    Died in 483 BC, aged 80
Muhammad (Founder of Islam)
    Died in AD 632, aged 62
Karl Marx (The great mind behind Communism)
    Died in 1883, aged 64

Now compare *and contrast* Jesus Christ. He died in AD 30, as a young man in his thirties. He spent only three years in the public eye, and those were spent in a fairly remote place. When he died he left no writing, and only a few dispirited, demoralised followers.

Yet the impact of Jesus on history has been at least as great as that of the great men listed above. We don't set aside one day in the year to remember him by, as with most other great figures. We base our whole calendar on his life. Every time we write the date we pay an unconscious tribute to his birth. The essayist R. W. Emerson could say that the name of Jesus "is not so much written, as ploughed, into the history of the world."

Hans Küng sums up like this: "None of the great founders of religions lived in so restricted an area. None lived for such a terribly short time. None died so young. And yet how great his influence has been . . . Numerically, Christianity is well ahead of all world religions."

This is a fact which demands an explanation. How could this village carpenter turned preacher make such a colossal impact, given his short life?

Men continue to influence the world after they are dead in two ways: through their *writings*, and through their *followers*. Jesus left no writings. True, his short earthly life made a powerful impact on his disciples. But this was largely cancelled by the shattering blow caused by his early death. So how did he do it? The New Testament answer is that Jesus really did die on the cross – but God raised him from the dead. So Jesus is alive and he continues to influence events in the world, by his Spirit.

When we read of a satellite circling the earth, we know that it was not the explosion of a child's firework which put it there. A big fact requires a big explanation. The same is true here. The continuing influence of Jesus, the startling transformation in the disciples, and the beginning of the Christian movement which sprang from this, are "big" facts. They require a sufficiently "big" explanation. Resurrection is exactly the right size.

John Polkinghorne ponders the remarkable rise of the Church and concludes: "Something happened to bring it about. Whatever it was it must have been of a magnitude commensurate with the effect it produced. I believe that was the resurrection of Jesus from the dead."

Second fact: several people claimed that they saw the Risen Lord

One Easter Sunday, a clergyman in Ipswich came down from the pulpit and stood on his head. When young Willy Smith told his mother what the sermon was about, she could be excused for scolding him for telling stories.

It *was* an unusual event. We do not easily accept something like that on the evidence of a single witness. But if several people claim that they saw the same thing – including several older members of the Church whose honesty is tried and tested – what then? We would be forced to accept their word about that headstand.

The apostle Paul wrote a letter to the Christians in the Greek town of Corinth, about twenty-five years after the death of Jesus. In this letter he gave a list of people who claimed that they had seen the Lord, very much alive, after his death on the cross.

James was one. Peter was another. We can be quite certain of their honesty, for their teaching and writing were of the highest moral calibre. Besides, they were prepared to suffer and die for their beliefs (see Fact 3). Then there was the group of five hundred. Paul reminded his readers that most of these were still alive when he wrote. Their testimony could easily be checked.

We are right to view a report that someone has risen from the dead with deep suspicion. But if enough people claim to have seen him, and if other evidence points in the same direction, the situation changes. A continuing refusal to believe does not display a healthy suspicion about an unusual happening; it displays a refusal to face facts.

In his book *Jesus Christ: the Witness of History* Professor Sir Norman Anderson records a striking example of this. He relates a conversation with a professor of philosophy, who agreed that the evidence for Jesus' resurrection is strong. But he refused to accept the evidence because "it simply could not have happened"!

Third fact: the disciples suffered for their preaching

The men who deserted Jesus to save their skins went into hiding. Then, a few weeks later, they began to preach that God had raised Jesus from the dead. They were the same men who had been crushed and shattered by his crucifixion. They were the same men who had met in secret. But they were very different same men!

In place of bitter disappointment there was joyful certainty; in place of fear there was boldness; instead of hiding behind locked doors, they were out preaching to the crowds; instead of thinking gloomily that their leader was dead, they proclaimed that he had conquered death.

In other words, they were transformed. The question is:

what transformed them? They claimed that it was because God had raised Jesus from the dead. Were they right? Were they mistaken? Or were they guilty of the greatest fraud in history?

An invention? They had a motive for lying – to rescue the good name of their beloved teacher. We can imagine them plotting: "Let's steal the body, and say that God has raised him from the dead."

This neat solution founders on one fact. History teaches us that people will suffer for deeply held convictions. No one is prepared to suffer for something he has cooked up. We tell lies to get out of trouble, not to get into it! The whip and the sword soon uncover inventors. Besides, liars don't usually write high-calibre moral literature like the New Testament.

The willing suffering of the disciples also rules out the "swoon" theory. In this view, Jesus didn't die on the cross. Despite terrible wounds, he recovered in the tomb, and escaped. The disciples nursed him back to health, or tried to and failed.

This theory bristles with problems. Roman soldiers knew when a man was dead; and there was the guard on the tomb. But if we allow for a moment that this might have happened, the events which follow simply don't fit.

Jesus would have *cheated* death; he would not have *conquered* it. No doubt the disciples would have been delighted. But *they would have kept the whole thing very quiet*. Publicity and preaching would have been fatal, for it would have resulted in a search. The authorities would not have made a second mistake.

Besides, to preach that God had raised Jesus from the dead – which is exactly what they did preach – would have been a lie. We are back where we started. The lash, the dungeon and the sword would soon have loosened their tongues. Men will suffer and die for their *convictions*, but not for their *inventions*.

Fourth fact: hallucinations need certain conditions

One thing is certain. The first disciples passionately believed that Jesus had risen and that he had appeared to them. Were they mistaken? Perhaps they saw a ghost, or suffered from hallucinations?

Well, if it was a disembodied spirit, vision or a ghost, it spent a lot of time and energy trying to persuade them that it wasn't! The Risen Lord had extraordinary powers of appearance and disappearance. He didn't hide these, but he did convince the disciples that it was in his body – albeit remarkably transformed – that he came and went. They ate with him and touched him – and they concluded that God had raised him from the dead.

Perhaps the disciples were suffering from *hallucinations*? At first sight this seems more likely. But when we compare the factors involved in hallucinations with the appearances recorded in the Gospels, they don't fit. For one thing, hallucinations happen to individuals. Several people in a group – under the influence of drugs, for example – might hallucinate together. But they will experience *different* hallucinations, for these arise from the subconscious mind, and every individual's subconscious is as personal as his fingerprints.

In his book *The Day Death Died*, Michael Green sifts out six features attaching to hallucinations. Not one of these is present in the resurrection appearances. If these appearances were not inventions nor delusions, it is hard to escape the logical conclusion. As John Robinson put it: "HE came to them . . . Jesus was not a dead memory but a living presence, making new men of them."

Fifth fact: they preached resurrection, not resuscitation or survival

Professor James Dunn underlines this point in *The Evidence for Jesus*. Throughout history – including Jewish history – extraordinary happenings have convinced some people about life after death. For example, ancient Jewish literature speaks of people seeing visions of their dead heroes – heroes like Abel and Jeremiah. But as James Dunn points out: "In no other case did the one(s) seeing the vision conclude 'This man has been raised from the dead.'"

I do not want to put *too* much weight on this. After all, Jesus had told his disciples that he would rise again – even though they did not grasp what he was saying. Also, many Jews believed in resurrection – but in the resurrection of *all people* on the "last day", not of *one man* in the middle of history.

So it remains true that nothing in the thought-forms of the day led them to expect the resurrection appearances of Jesus to occur in the way in which the New Testament describes them. Like so many other factors surrounding Jesus, the events are unique and unexpected. Invention of this particular story is highly improbable, because they were not that clever.

Sixth fact: no one produced the body

The Church began, not primarily by the spreading of ideas, but by the proclamation of a fact. Something has *happened*, said the Apostles. Jesus has risen from the grave.

To disprove an idea you must argue. To disprove a fact, you must produce evidence. Those who wanted to discredit the Apostles – and the Jewish leaders wanted to do that very much indeed – had only to produce one piece of evidence to make the disciples look very silly.

All they had to do was to produce the body of Jesus. *If they had done that we would never have heard of him*, or of his followers. There would be no Church.

It is very significant that they could not do this. If the authorities had taken the body, or discovered it still in the tomb – because the disciples had lied, or had gone to the wrong grave – they would have produced the corpse. When Peter and the rest began preaching that God had raised Jesus, this would have silenced them instantly.

Instead, the authorities imprisoned, threatened, and beat the disciples. And they circulated the report that the disciples had stolen the body. It is absolutely certain that the Jewish and Roman leaders had no idea at all what had happened to Jesus. Yet the stubborn fact remains: his body had gone.

Seventh fact: the tomb was not venerated

The empty tomb is strongly supported by the fact that the grave of Jesus did not become a place of pilgrimage. Tomb veneration was common at the time of Jesus, and people would often meet for worship at the grave of a dead prophet – as they do today.

In surprising contrast, the earliest Jewish Christians did no such thing. "*No* practice of tomb veneration, or even of meeting for worship at Jesus' tomb is attested for the first Christians," affirms Professor Dunn. Veneration of the *empty* tomb began two or three hundred years later – and it persists today.

That the tomb of Jesus did not become a place of pilgrimage for the first Christians has only one satisfactory explanation. "The tomb was not venerated, it did not become a place of pilgrimage, because the tomb was empty!" (James Dunn)

Eighth fact: they called Jesus "Lord"

The first disciples were Jews – devout monotheists who frequently recited the Shema: "The LORD our God, the LORD is one" (Deut. 6:4). Then they met Jesus. At no point did they abandon their belief in the One God. It would have been unthinkable for them to become bi-theists (believers in two Gods), yet their concept of God was greatly enlarged as a result of their contact with Jesus. So, while continuing to assert that God is One, they began to speak of God the Father and of God the Son. Within a short period of time they had firmly placed Jesus, the man from Nazareth, on the Godward side of that line which divides humanity from divinity.

When the early Christians called Jesus "Lord", they were not politely addressing him as "Sir". No. They were applying to Jesus the name used for God in the Greek translation of the Hebrew Bible (our Old Testament).

How can this amazing shift in attitude be explained? How can we account for the fact that these Jewish men and women, some of whom knew Jesus of Nazareth personally, and all of whom knew that he was a man who sweated and wept, could nevertheless address him as Lord (i.e. God)?

It was not deep philosophical analysis which led them to this conclusion; it was reflection upon their puzzling and startling experiences. Above all, it was their conviction that God had raised Jesus from the dead. For if Jesus was Lord over life and death, he was, quite simply . . . LORD.

Ninth fact: modern psychology supports it

By this I don't mean that most psychologists agree about the resurrection. I mean that the considerable amount of modern knowledge about the way in which people behave under stress points to it.

I was ordained alongside a man who was for many years a high-ranking officer in the RAF. He explained to me how he became a convinced Christian in the first place. He was recovering from flu, and having nothing much to read, he picked up a copy of a new translation of the New Testament which his wife had bought. He began to read, and it gripped him. When he eventually put that Bible down, he was certain of one thing: the resurrection of Jesus is a fact. He saw that this was the only possible explanation for the incredible change which took place in the disciples.

He was an experienced leader. During the war he was awarded the Distinguished Flying Cross, and he had been a prisoner under the Japanese as a very young man. He understood well how people behave under stress. He knew that dispirited people aren't creative people. He knew that men do not reassemble and organise themselves effectively, after the sort of crushing disappointment which Jesus' disciples had experienced.

A handful of frightened men would not suddenly preach boldly to the very people who had killed their leader – and so risk their own lives. People just do not behave like that – *unless something tremendous happens to drive away the fear and disappointment.*

That wing commander was convinced that in the case of the disciples, the necessary "something" must have happened. Jesus really *must* have appeared to them after rising from the dead. That discovery set in motion the process which was to revolutionise his life.

Tenth fact: Christ's power today

One surprising feature of the reported resurrection appearances is that they were confined to a period of six weeks. After that they stopped abruptly. Yet the first disciples continued to speak and behave as though Jesus was with them – not physically, but by his Spirit.

Even more remarkable is the fact that this conviction was shared by others – at first by hundreds, then thousands, then millions – who had never seen Jesus, before or after his crucifixion.

The evidence is not confined to the past. Thousands of men and women continue to experience a new power, and a continuing "presence" in their lives. Although of differing backgrounds, cultures, ages and temperaments, they put it down to the same cause: the Risen Lord is alive and at work in our world today.

The actor James Fox is an example of this. He was one of the "beautiful people" of the swinging sixties. He featured in several films: *Those Magnificent Men in Their Flying Machines; Thoroughly Modern Millie; Performance.* His life sounds like a cliché of the period: drugs, sex, fame and wealth.

Yet he was confused, and frightened of losing control of his life. Fitfully he read the New Testament and attended church. On Christmas Day 1968, by a series of unlikely coincidences, he met an enthusiastic Christian over breakfast in a hotel. They talked without embarrassment about the love of God, and the way of salvation. James Fox became a Christian – then he became a salesman, an estate agent, and a full-time Christian worker.

After a ten-year break he picked up the threads of his acting career. He records all this in his book, *Comeback* – described by Dirk Bogarde as "moving, and searingly honest". To summarise in a way which I think James Fox would approve: he met the living, Risen Lord, who turned his life the right way up.

Eleventh fact: the evidence convinces some surprising people

Two Jewish scholars have recently studied the evidence for the resurrection and – given their background – they have come to a remarkable conclusion. In *Jesus the Jew* Geza Vermes writes:

> When every argument has been considered and weighed, the only conclusion acceptable to the historian must be . . . that the women who set out to pay their last respects to Jesus found to their consternation, not a body, but an empty tomb.

In 1985 an orthodox Jewish scholar – Professor Pinchas Lapide – wrote a book entitled *The Resurrection of Jesus*. He surveys the evidence and concludes: "I accept the resurrection of Jesus not as an invention of the community of disciples, but as a historical event."

More than once in this book I have conceded that Christianity isn't a "tidy" religion. It is coherent and (in my view) it has the "ring of truth". But it presents us with problems and loose ends. So I am suspicious when the package presented for our inspection is *too* neat. However, I am convinced that there are few significant loose ends as far as the resurrection of Jesus is concerned – apart from our own inability or unwillingness to believe such a stupendous event.

Leslie Weatherhead likened our examination of the evidence to a journey. When all the signposts point to a particular village, then we are foolish to deny that the village exists, just because we haven't been there. If this particular village does exist – if God really *did* raise Jesus from the dead – then our own life and death begin to take on a totally new significance.

Jesus has defeated death. He is the first fruits of a great harvest. *We* are that harvest. He has thrown wide open the gate of glory. Heaven awaits. Our present life is the shadow; life in the world to come is the substance (1 John 3: 1–3).

We have been sifting evidence so I will invite a lawyer – Sir Edward Clarke – to have the last word:

> As a lawyer I have made a prolonged study of the evidence for the events of the first Easter Day. To me the evidence is conclusive, and over and over again in the High Court I have secured the verdict on evidence not nearly so compelling . . . as a lawyer I accept it unreservedly as the testimony of truthful men to facts they were able to substantiate.

17

Five into One Won't Go

Before moving on we need to face one further problem for belief in the resurrection – the differences in the five accounts of the resurrection appearances in the New Testament (four in the Gospels, plus 1 Corinthians 15).

Everyone agrees that these accounts pose problems, for it is not easy to put the five together and come up with a single tidy narrative. The most recent attempt to do so has been made by John Wenham in *Easter Enigma*. (He is better known to those embarking on a study of theology by a less popular book: *Elements of New Testament Greek!*) John Wenham's book is based on a deep knowledge of modern scholarship – and of modern Israel, where he once lived.

At the other end of the spectrum are scholars who write off the task as useless. In their view it is impossible to harmonise the five accounts. Without going into details, I will make three points.

1.   The evidence for the resurrection does not depend upon reducing the five accounts to one harmonious whole. Indeed, the evidence for the resurrection doesn't depend upon the finer details of the New Testament at all. It depends on something much bigger than this – finding a satisfactory explanation for the remarkable growth of the Christian Church in such poor soil.

Given the dejection of the disciples when Jesus died, together with the fact that he left no writing, the rise of the Christian movement was impossible – without a transforming factor. Those same disciples were responsible for an unparalleled burst of creative, joyful energy. This is a fact which cries out for adequate explanation.

Professor C. F. D. Moule of Cambridge summed up like this: "If the coming into existence of the Nazarenes (i.e. the Christian Church) . . . rips a great hole in history, a hole of the size and shape of resurrection, what does the secular historian propose to stop it up with?"

2.   Honest witnesses usually give different accounts of the same event – whether they are describing an accident, or a visit to the seaside, or anything else. Of course, if the accounts have a different *centre*, we are suspicious. Equally, if the descriptions are very similar, we suspect collusion.

The New Testament accounts of the events surrounding the resurrection ring true. One feature is certainly not invented. *The Gospels agree that the first witnesses were women.* In today's Iran, the testimony of a woman carries less weight than a man's testimony. A similar viewpoint was adopted in the culture of Jesus. The Evangelists wanted to convince their contemporaries, but they weren't prepared to cook the books by excluding the women. "Weak" evidence like this has all the hallmarks of honesty.

3.   There is a need for humility when reconstructing events at a long distance. I sometimes wonder what future historians would make of the patchy diaries of a student in England in our own century. The diary tells us that he enjoyed good health, and that he started school at Christ's *Hospital*, before

transferring to Clifton *College* in Bristol. After that he went to
university at the London *School* of Economics.

Bold minds in 2,000 years time would reconstruct his life.
Clearly his statement about good health was wishful thinking,
for he spent a year in hospital. And the dates which he gave for
Bristol and London are muddled, for twentieth-century boys
attended school *before* going to college, not the other way
round. Wiser heads would counsel caution, knowing that
partial information can mislead.

I will end with one very wise head from our own century.
Commenting on the apparently muddled state of the accounts
of the resurrection appearances, the playwright Dorothy
Sayers wrote:

> The divergences appear very great on first sight . . . But the
> fact remains that *all* of them, without exception, can be made
> to fall into place in a single orderly and coherent narrative
> without the smallest contradiction or difficulty, and without
> any suppression, invention, or manipulation, beyond a
> trifling effort to *imagine* the natural behaviour of a bunch
> of startled people running about in the dawnlight between
> Jerusalem and the Garden.

TAKE A BREAK (6)

A vicar was surprised to receive a phone call asking him to
visit the home of Mrs. Jones, who was ill in bed. He was
surprised because the Joneses were a staunch Chapel family.
But he was glad of an opportunity to improve Church/Chapel
relationships, and as it was August, he assumed that the
Baptist minister was on holiday.

At the end of his visit he told the family how sorry he was
that their own minister was away during their time of need.
"Oh he's not away," replied Mr. Jones. "We called you because
we thought the illness might be contagious."

*   *   *

The above reminds me of a wedding story which is believable
(because people do sometimes behave very strangely in
church) but unverifiable.

During a wedding service, the happy couple were kneeling at the chancel steps when the rector whispered, "And now follow me to the Communion rail." He walked the fifteen paces fairly slowly, then looked round. To his surprise they were following him as he requested – by shuffling on their knees.

*   *   *

From a Parish Magazine (so it must be true!): The best man ran into problems when he came to sign the Marriage Register in the vestry at Cawthorne, Yorkshire. The pen wouldn't write, so the vicar offered some advice (as vicars often do!). "Put your weight on it," he said. When he read the entry he was surprised to see: John Smith (10 stone 4 lb.).

*   *   *

From the Letters columns (of a magazine): Until my son was four, we spent every Sunday visiting my aged father. When he died, we were able to start going to church. When a neighbour asked if we'd take her little boy to Sunday School with us, my son replied, "Oh no, he can't go to church till he's got relatives in heaven!" Further questioning revealed that he thought we were going to church so that we could talk to his grandpa. He'd been praying, "Grandfather, which art in heaven . . ." (M.P.D., Swansea).

*   *   *

"When you die, God takes care of you like your mother did when you were alive – only God doesn't yell at you all the time" (Steve K, age 8).

*   *   *

A Welshman dreamed that he went to heaven. "In my dream," he said, "I saw heaven as a vast choir. In the front row, stretching from east to west, there was a vast number of sopranos. Behind them, an equal number of altos. Behind them, a similarly huge crowd of tenors. And behind them, in the back row, there was *me*, singing bass all alone.

St. Peter raised his baton, and we sang "Guide me O thou great Redeemer". It was beautiful. But St. Peter wasn't satisfied; the balance wasn't quite right. So he tapped his baton and we stopped. Then St. Peter looked up, pointed at me and said, "A little less bass, please."

*   *   *

The Church Business meeting moved to Item 5 on the Agenda: "Purchase of Candelabra". One long-standing member stood up – a man who occasionally got hold of the wrong end of the stick. "I'm against this idea," he declared. "For one thing, we have just overhauled the organ. For another thing, no one in the church can play a candelabra. In any case, if we have any spare funds, we should concentrate on improving the lighting in the church."

Part VI

Prove it! Does God exist?

We die on the day
when our lives cease to be
illumined
by the steady radiance
renewed daily,
of a wonder,
the source of which
is beyond reason.
Dag Hammarskjold

God often visits us, but most of the time we are not at home.
French Proverb

I cannot prove the existence of God, but neither can I watch a
symphony orchestra at work, and believe that there is no
benevolent purpose to the Creation.

Gordon McGregor

18

This Amazing Universe

Does God exist? This apparently abstract question can be very practical. A young married woman wrote to a newspaper with a problem. Should she and her husband remain faithful to each other, to provide a strong family unit for their children?

It was a serious question. Would the couple find greater fulfilment by taking several "lovers"? If that woman believed that God has given us laws for our guidance and obedience – including the commandment "You shall not commit adultery" (Exod. 20:14) – she would find an answer to her very practical question.

A man who became an alcoholic and a tramp spoke movingly about his downward slide. It began as a result of guilt feelings when he became father to his girlfriend's baby. If he believed in a forgiving and merciful God, that man's life would have been very different.

No opting out: We cannot opt out of belief. Faith does not involve believing six impossible things before breakfast. Christians are called "believers", but *all* people base their lives on assumptions which cannot be proved with mathematical certainty. The Christian *believes* that God exists. The atheist *believes* that God does not exist. The agnostic *believes* that there is insufficient evidence to decide one way or the other. The indifferent person *believes* that it does not matter either way.

A high-ranking Russian defector gave a radio interview during the days of the Soviet Union. "When I was young, when I joined the foreign ministry, I was a believer," he declared. It was when he ceased to believe in Marxism that he came to the West.

It is not a question of *whether* we believe but *what* we believe – and whether our beliefs are backed up by the available evidence. For not all acts of faith are equally well placed. Bookmakers base their livelihood on the fact that some acts of faith have more evidence to support them than others. Which is why some horses run at 100–1, and others are odds-on favourites.

What about belief in God? Is there any evidence to support this act of faith? Many reasons for faith in God have been given during human history – and in the course of this book. It is time to draw the threads together. From this mass of ideas, I will concentrate on three important areas. In this chapter we shall consider the natural world – our incredible universe.

We find evidence of order and design in the universe. Where there is design, there must be a Designer. That Designer, we call God. This sums up the famous Argument from Design (called the Teleological Argument by philosophers). We will examine the two parts of the argument.

1. Is there evidence of design?

A woman looked through a microscope. What she saw was so beautiful that she thought it was a diamond. In fact she was looking at the eye of a water flea – a striking combination of utility and beauty. But it can be argued that organs like eyes have resulted from thousands of years of adaptation to the environment. So another form of this argument has been developed, which concentrates on things which cannot adapt.

A large number of factors in our world are just right to support life. If the earth was much smaller there would be insufficient gravity to hold air around our planet. If the moon was much nearer or much bigger, we should suffer from massive tidal waves, caused by its gravitational pull. If we were nearer to the sun we would fry. If we were further away we would freeze. (In fact, of course, there would be no "we"!)

The *stability* of our atmosphere is a key factor. Recently I heard a scientist puzzling over this. He was surprised that the balance of gases has remained so remarkably stable over such a long period. If the balance *did* vary, we would face enormous problems. A little less oxygen than 20.9 per cent would make breathing difficult; rather more and numerous forest fires would break out. The right balance continues – probably due to the vast network of living, breathing organisms. But – as every child knows – experts warn that our modern way of life might inflict mortal damage on our life-supporting environment.

Another factor which is "just right" is water. This vital substance has remarkable properties. It dissolves a very large number of substances (I am told that in the blood it holds over 60 substances in solution). It is not easily decomposed. It boils and freezes at temperatures which are ideally suited to the wide temperature range of our planet.

Water has extraordinary properties when nearing its freezing point. As it cools below 4°C, water *expands* – unlike other fluids, which contract. This is vital for water creatures in cold temperatures. For without this property ice would not form on the *top* of pools and rivers, but from the bottom. The expansion of water on freezing is also important for soil production – and hence vegetation – because it breaks up rocks. It is less good for lead water pipes, for the same reason!

Clearly then, a very large number of remarkable factors has come together to support life on earth. In many ways our world is strikingly beautiful and orderly. Which is not to say that *everything* is harmonious and well ordered. We have already noted the fact of *dis*harmony and the problems this raises, in Chapter 13.

2. Must there be a Designer?

Does all this mean that there must be a Designer? Unfortunately not.

It means that there *may* be a Designer. Perhaps it means that there *probably is* a Designer. But we cannot use the phrase "there must be". There is another option open to us. We may look at the universe, and maintain that it is the work of blind, mindless *chance* – things just happened to work out right. Those who believe this often say that it is the *disharmony* (suffering, earthquakes, etc.) which leads them to this view.

Some people look at the universe and say "I believe in God." Despite the areas of disharmony, they maintain that only God can account for breathtaking beauty, for conscience and for the incredible number of things which work together to make life possible.

Other people look at the universe and say "I believe in chance." It is open to them to make this act of faith. Pattern, order and surprises (like the properties of water) cannot prove beyond all doubt that God exists. The argument for God's existence, based on design in the universe, may be strong, but it is not watertight.

If we are to get beyond the point of stalemate we must look elsewhere. In particular we must consider personal experience, and history.

CONCLUDING QUOTATIONS

In my judgment the convergence of all these factors makes it far, far more probable that God does exist than that he does not – *Bishop Hugh Montefiore*.

The ancient covenant is in pieces; man at last knows that he is alone in the unfeeling vastness of the universe, out of which he emerged by chance. Neither his destiny nor his duty have been written down – *Jacques Monod*.

The universe is full of the clatter of monkeys playing with typewriters, but once they have hit on the first line of *Hamlet* it seems that they are marvellously constrained to continue to the end of at least some sort of play – *John Polkinghorne*.

19

Evidence from Personal Experience

A wide range of personal experiences convince people of the existence of God. I will outline and illustrate some of these.

1. General experience of the world

Geoffrey Smith is a familiar voice on radio and television – to gardening enthusiasts at least. Like many farmers and gardeners he has a strong "intuition" or "instinct" which convinces him of the existence of a Creator. The view that this world – with its abundance of life and growth – came about by chance is, to him, quite incredible.

He reminds me of another gardener: a man whose knowledge of the soil leaves him with a deep sense of wonder and gratitude – and with a sense of humour. He wryly tells the story of the gardener and the squire. "It's marvellous what you and the good Lord have accomplished between you," said the squire as he surveyed the scene. "Aye," said the gardener, "but you should have seen what it was like when the good Lord had it to himself"!

2. Particular experiences of God

Frances Young is a university teacher and a mother. She teaches theology, and returns home to a severely handicapped son. In her professional life she grapples with the theological problems presented by a world in which things go badly wrong. In her private life she lives with the practical problems arising from this same fact (although I suspect that she would not describe her son as "a problem").

Frances is a radical, probing theologian. She has a colleague who recently lost his faith in God. She knows that there are no knock-down arguments for the existence of God. Yet she speaks with deep conviction of her own faith – and about certain experiences which convince her of the reality of a personal God.

One day she was sitting in a chair when she had a "loud thought". It was as though a voice said to her: "It doesn't make any difference to Me whether you believe in Me or not!" Later, when driving her car she had another "loud thought" telling her to be ordained. She can't remember the journey itself ("I must have been on automatic pilot or something"), but she remembers the experience very clearly.

"I had the whole of my life laid out in front of me; and all its peculiar twists and turns which hadn't seemed to make very much sense suddenly fell into a pattern, as though this was all leading up to that moment and that conclusion. It was quite dramatic in its way." Frances was ordained as a minister in the Methodist Church on 3rd July, 1984.

The late Gerald Priestland, who recorded these experiences in *The Case Against God*, confessed to similar experiences of his own. He admitted that "none of this can be demonstrated or transferred to anyone else, nor can anyone else persuade the experiencer that it is a delusion. In an odd way it is more real than a letter or a telephone call that could be shared." He summed up his position in two short sentences: "I hope I believe. I know that I trust."

He also described the fascinating research into religious experience at the Research Unit based in Oxford. It is clear that more people have experiences of this kind than we might imagine – although they are often rather shy about them. 36 per cent of those questioned in a recent door-to-door survey admitted to having experiences of this sort.

3. Direct experiences of Jesus

Some people are convinced that they have "met" Jesus. Fred Lemon was a criminal: vicious, greedy and devious. One day, after a spell in the punishment block, and while he was planning a murder in his prison cell, he had three visitors. He is convinced that one of them was Jesus.

He describes this remarkable incident in his book *Break-out*, and he adds:

> When he'd gone there was this tremendous feeling that I was worth something after all; that with his help I could be the sort of person he wanted me to be. There was a great peace in my heart; it gave me the sleep of a little child . . .

The result of this encounter was a revolution in Fred's life. He left prison, and set up an open, caring home with his wife Doris – who had remained loyal to Fred through all those difficult years. They adopted five needy children. Fred became a greengrocer, thus fulfilling St. Paul's instruction to converted thieves:

> He who has been stealing must steal no longer, but must work, doing something useful with his own hands, that he may have something to share with those in need (Eph. 4:28).

Archbishop Anthony Bloom enjoyed a varied and distinguished career: as a surgeon, a member of the wartime resistance movement, and as a leader of the Russian Orthodox Church in Britain. In upbringing, culture and learning he is utterly different from Fred Lemon. But as a young man he had an experience very like Fred's.

Having heard a lecture on Christianity he was angry, and he began to read St. Mark's Gospel in order to prove that it was false. (He chose St. Mark because it was the shortest, and he

didn't want to waste time on the exercise!) He relates what
happened next in his book *School For Prayer*:

> Before I reached the third chapter, I suddenly became aware
> that on the other side of my desk there was a presence. And
> the certainty was so strong that it was Christ standing there
> that it has never left me. This was the real turning point.
> Because Christ was alive and I had been in his presence I
> could say with certainty that what the Gospel said about the
> crucifixion of the prophet of Galilee was true, and the
> centurion was right when he said, "Truly he is the Son of
> God."

That experience had a profound effect upon the subsequent
shape of his life. A deep conviction of the reality of the risen
Christ has stayed with him ever since.

What are we to make of such reports? Certainly, I have never
had such an experience, and because I have a large chunk of
scepticism in my make-up, I look for alternative explanations.
But I know Fred Lemon – he seems to me to have a well-
balanced, tough personality. And having heard and read
Anthony Bloom, I am struck by his deep sanity and inner
stillness. They may be mistaken, but I doubt that they are
given to hallucinations. And I am certain that they are honest
witnesses. It is not easy to explain their experiences away.

4. Remarkable coincidences

Michael Bourdeaux is an English clergyman who speaks fluent
Russian. He founded Keston College, a research unit devoted to
helping believers in Communist lands. The way in which he
was "directed" into this work is striking. In 1963 he received a
letter, via Paris, in semi-literate Russian. The letter was not
addressed to him. It was passed to him because it described the
fierce persecutions under Khruschev (for example, some active
Christians were confined in mental asylums).

The following year he went to Moscow, and visited the
Church of St. Peter and Paul, only to find that it had been

destroyed by order of the authorities. As he looked at the rubble, two elderly women were doing the same. At this point I will let Michael himself take up the story.

I addressed them in Russian. They could not have reacted more sharply if I had touched them with an electrified wire. "Oh! If you're afraid to talk, I'll leave you at once."

"Who are you?"

"I'm a foreigner come here to find out about the church."

In a second, the hand had commissioned me. They bade me follow them – trolley, tram, a walk in the distant suburbs, an upstairs room.

"Why really did you come?"

"I had heard the persecution was so much worse."

"Who told you that?"

"I received a letter . . . from Paris."

"Who wrote it?"

Hesitating, I named the two signatories.

Silence . . . a sudden flood of uncontrolled sobbing. "We wrote that letter . . . we've come to Moscow today for the second time to make contact with someone again. God sent you to meet us."

To summarise: the women had travelled seven hundred miles from their home, and Michael Bourdeaux had flown from England. Several months earlier those women had sent a letter to France which had been passed to this Englishman, of whom neither of them had heard. The writers of the letter and its recipient would not have met had either of them arrived at the demolished church an hour earlier or later.

We begin to see what Archbishop William Temple meant when he commented that when he stopped praying, coincidences stopped happening! Following their plea for help, Michael Bourdeaux launched his life's work – careful research into the facts concerning life for believers (Jewish, Muslim, Buddhist and Christian) in Communist lands. His work has been crucial to those suffering persecution.

5. Healings

In *The Oak and the Calf*, Alexander Solzhenitsyn describes his despair at being told that – because of cancer – he had three weeks to live. He had much to tell the world and he feared that the Soviet authorities would discover and destroy his writings. Desperately he hid his work. That was in 1953. In 1970 he was awarded the Nobel Prize for Literature! He comments, "With a hopelessly neglected and acutely malignant tumour, this was a divine miracle; I could see no other explanation. Since then, all the life that has been given back to me has not been mine in the full sense: it is built around a purpose."

In the *British Medical Journal*, (Dec. 1983) Dr. Rex Gardner describes four recent healings, which parallel miracles recorded by the Venerable Bede twelve centuries ago. It is a detailed and impressive article. Dr. Gardner tells of the full recovery of a young doctor who became so ill that she was expected to die, but for whom several prayer groups were formed. Dr. Gardner wrote: "Physicians were unable to explain how her chest X-ray film, which had showed extensive left-sided pneumonia with collapse of the middle lobe, could, 48 hours later, show a normal clear chest."

The debate about miraculous healings came into sharp focus in 1992 and 1993 following the London meetings of the American preacher, Morris Cerullo. He claimed that many such healings took place. This claim was challenged by Dr. Peter May, a Christian doctor, who asserted that medical evidence for healing claims should be produced. This important debate continues.

To be personal, I must admit that I don't live in a world where this kind of thing is common, but even I get surprises. I recall receiving a letter from a woman with whom I had prayed at Scargill House (a Christian centre in the Yorkshire Dales), following her course of radiotherapy. Her suspected cancer has been cured, and she believes that God has healed her through medical science and prayer. Doubters will no doubt see this as a shrewd means of hedging one's bets!

I think too of Anne, a Christian probation officer who suffered from the scourge of multiple sclerosis. She now seems very fit, and firmly believes that God has gradually healed her through prayer and the laying on of hands. Others will rightly point out that multiple sclerosis is sometimes "like that". It comes and goes; it can lie dormant for years. Anne discerns the hand of God, but proof is out of the question. Doctors sometimes use the term "spontaneous remission" for unexpected recovery (in cancer, for example). Perhaps this is a secular term for a miracle. In the nature of things we can never be certain.

I do know several people – intelligent, honest people – who claim (often in a matter-of-fact way) that they have witnessed wonderful, apparently miraculous healings, following prayer. I am convinced by their testimony.

The words of the saintly Oxford scholar Austin Farrer are worth weighing: "The miracles of the saints never cease: a hundred years ago the sainted Cure d'Ars multiplied bread and healed the sick and lived himself by a continuous physical miracle, nor has he lacked successors since."

Of course, we all know that people sometimes pray, and remain ill or die. It would be cruel, foolish and false to suggest that lack of healing indicates a lack of faith, or the judgment of God.

It is my conviction that miracles do sometimes happen to some people. If so, this is clear evidence of the existence – and of the activity – of God. But on occasions, in his perfect wisdom, it seems that God answers our prayers with other words than "Yes". Words like "Wait" or "No" – as he did to Jesus (Mark 14:36) and St. Paul (2 Cor 12:8,9).

6. Experiences of God through suffering

A widow was only just recovering from the death of her husband when she had another terrible blow: her first grand-daughter was still-born. Her two Christian daughters encouraged their mother to pray. One night she followed their advice, and the next morning she woke up with a sense of inner healing and peace. It was as though her life had begun again. She began to experience "the peace of God which passes all understanding" (Phil. 4:7, RSV).

Sometimes God's presence seems to bring strength rather

than peace. That was certainly the experience of Bishop Wilson of Singapore as he was tortured (see page 118). He received strength in two ways: strength to *endure* and strength to *forgive*.

Such experiences are not uncommon among Christians, but they are by no means universal. C. S. Lewis wrote a diary to enable him to cope with his grief when his wife died. He admits that he sometimes felt desolate and alone.

He did not write glowingly about experiencing God's presence. But he recalled Jesus' cry of dereliction on the cross: "My God, my God, why have you forsaken me?" He came to see more deeply into St. Paul's affirmation (2 Cor. 5:7) that we are called to walk by faith, not by sight – nor, ultimately, by feelings and emotions, either.

Sometimes the courage of those who suffer is tremendously moving. A friend who was forced to take early retirement as a result of multiple sclerosis wrote:

> I've had to give up driving. The fatigue is rotten, but not such a worry now that I've stopped working.
>
> The blurred and double/triple vision is a nuisance, but curiously interesting, e.g. the Cathedral has had 2 spires for a couple of years; there are 3 moons in the sky and an awful lot of 8-legged cats about!
>
> I am quite used to it now and it's not a worry.
>
> I've made no retirement plans, confident that something will emerge for me, when the time is right.

One of the most remarkable experiences of comfort and strength through prayer is recorded by Irina Ratushinskaya. In a freezing Soviet labour camp she – and others – sometimes experienced physical warmth and inner joy. In a poem she gave her "explanation". "Someone is thinking of me now. Petitioning the Lord for me".

7. Encounters with holiness

Michael Dummett was, until recently, Professor of Philosophy at Oxford University. He took over from one of England's best-known atheists – Professor Sir "Freddie" Ayer – who admired his successor's mind and ability, but strongly disagreed with his Christian Faith!

One reason which convinces Professor Dummett is that he finds truly holy people within the Church. Alas, not every Christian, by any means. But some people have a depth, a serenity and a joyful goodness which points him to God. John Polkinghorne makes a similar point in his book *The Way The World Is*:

> I have to say that in my experience most of the people I know who impress me most as being open to reality, deep in perception, firm in love, are also Christian believers. Of course, not all. I gladly acknowledge these qualities in friends who stand outside the faith. But there does seem to be a special quality in people who live close to God.

8. Friendship

Related to this is the remarkable experience of Christian friendship. I am extremely fortunate in having many fine friends. Some are believers; some are not. I am bound to say that I am struck by the fact that friendships with fellow Christians often (not always) achieve greater depths. There is a spirit of joyful, mutual understanding, which arises from sharing a common faith.

The New Testament often talks in corporate terms. Christian disciples do not pursue a lonely pilgrimage. *Together* they form the body of Christ, and the family of God. This actually works out in experience. Phrases like "in Christ", "brotherly love" and "fellowship in the Holy Spirit" are not clichés. Even though we often fail, and relationships sometimes break down, the depth of many Christian friendships points to the reality of their conviction that their unseen, Risen Lord is the most important person within the group.

Bishop Stephen Neill was a Christian leader and teacher in many continents, over many decades. Shortly before his death in 1984, he testified movingly to the enduring quality of friendships made across the world. He concluded: ". . . perhaps Christians are right in thinking that Jesus revealed new dimensions of friendship, and that he is himself the element of permanence in friendship between those who believe in him" (from *The Supremacy of Jesus*).

I recognise that these are a dangerous couple of paragraphs. They may seem suffocatingly "cosy" to those outside the Faith. If so, I am sorry. But I have decided to take the risk, for over the years the force of this experience has struck me time and again. And I am aware that this section will ring bells for many Christians who have never had a "remarkable" religious experience.

9. Undramatic experiences

At this point, space requires that I draw this chapter to a close. Selection has been inescapable, but I hope I have given enough examples to enable you to weigh up this aspect of the evidence for the existence and activity of God.

Perhaps it will ring bells in your experience. Perhaps it will not. I have described some remarkable examples, and this might be a mistake. For many people have a strong faith in God without undergoing dramatic experiences. For some, the main pointer is a quiet confidence that they are "accompanied", "helped" and "directed" through life by an unseen Presence – and challenged, too, to acts of love and service.

No doubt the material in this chapter will drive some readers to put this book down, and to reach for a manual in psychology or sociology! Even there you might not be quite safe. Peter Berger, a leading American sociologist, has written a brilliant book (*A Rumour of Angels*) in which he suggests that ordinary experiences like fear, comfort, hope and humour, point to God.

A good deal of what I have said can be summed up in one short sentence from the Gospels. "For where two or three come together in my name, there am I with them" (Matt. 18:20). Millions of ordinary believers, who have never had a "special" experience of God, will testify that these words of Jesus sum up their experience. They stubbornly affirm that they meet for prayer, worship and fellowship, not to remember a dead hero, but to meet – *and to be met by* – a living Person. Their testimony is impressive.

CONCLUDING EXPERIENCES

In his autobiography, Lord Clark (who died in 1980) described a religious experience. It is both moving and sad, and it shows that such experiences require a response. It also shows that refusal to respond is, in itself, a form of response.

> I had a religious experience. It took place in the Church of San Lorenzo, but did not seem to be connected with the harmonious beauty of the architecture. I can only say that for a few minutes my whole being was irradiated by a kind of heavenly joy, far more intense than anything I had known before. This state of mind lasted for several months, and, wonderful though it was, it posed an awkward problem in terms of action. My life was far from blameless: I would have to reform. My family would think I was going mad, and perhaps after all, it *was* a delusion, for I was in every way unworthy of receiving such a flood of grace. Gradually the effect wore off, and I made no effort to retain it. I think I was right; I was too deeply embedded in the world to change course. But that I had "felt the finger of God" I am quite sure, and, although the memory of this experience has faded, it still helps me to understand the joys of the saints – *From:* The Other Half: A Self-Portrait, *Kenneth Clark: 1977 (Page 108).*

Note: In fact, towards the end of his life, Lord Clark was received into the Roman Catholic Church.

* * *

To feed her addiction to drugs, Mary became a clever thief. By the time I met her, she had given up both drugs and theft and she was a lovely Christian in her mid-twenties.

I asked her what had happened. Has she woken one morning and decided to turn over a new leaf and make a new start? She smiled and pointed out that when you are on your face in the gutter, you can't get up, however hard you try. She lacked the moral vision and the spiritual strength to put her own life in order – but she went on to speak about the forgiveness and strength which she had received from the Risen Lord.

20

Evidence from History

Those who have known experiences of the kind I have just described find them compelling. To them they provide unshakeable evidence for the existence of God. But those to whom such experiences are foreign often find these accounts less convincing. So we move now to the third strand of evidence, which is, I believe, strongest of all.

By "the evidence from history" I mean especially those events which took place in the middle decades of what we now call the first century AD or CE. The evidence is not confined to those years – but it is at its strongest there. All we need to do at this point is briefly to recap four previous chapters (14–17).

1 In the course of his teaching, Jesus made far-reaching claims about himself. Despite this, his life-style was simple, and his manner was humble. He rings true. Here is no boaster, puffing himself up. On the contrary, he is more interested in serving than in being served. In particular, he wants to reach

out to the ordinary people of his day, and to outcasts (tax-collectors, prostitutes) regarded as beyond the pale.

All the evidence points strongly in one direction. Jesus is indeed the unique Son of God. If he *is*, then the God of whom he is the Son, must exist. Hence the question "Does God exist?" resolves itself into a question about Jesus. Equally important, the vital questions "What is God like?" and "Does God care?" do the same. For Jesus is a living "visual aid". He points us to God. He is a window into God. "No one has ever seen God, but the only begotten Son . . . has made him known" (John 1:18). Like Father, like Son. The keynote of his character is strong love.

The phrase "Sons of God" is also used in the New Testament to refer to those who – through faith in Jesus as the Risen Lord – have entered the family of God. But there is a clear difference between these two uses of the term. It is *his* sonship which makes *ours* possible. We are God's children "by adoption" (Rom. 8).

If we reject Jesus' own estimate of himself, we run into severe problems. The difficulty of finding a satisfactory alternative explanation for his teaching is tremendous. It might be possible for me to imagine that I am the world's greatest footballer – brilliant, but unrecognised – and to remain sane. It would be totally impossible to believe falsely that I have a unique relationship with God the Father, and a mission of incomparable significance, and to remain sane.

Either we accept Jesus' own estimate of himself – and hence accept that God exists – or we must write him off as a liar, or as a madman. His character, behaviour, and moral teaching, make these last two explanations extremely difficult to accept. To get round the problem, we invent a fourth category. Jesus is not divine; nor was he a liar or a madman. He was a good man and a great teacher – and nothing more. But this is a mirage. It will not stand up under investigation.

On one occasion, because of his hard teaching, large numbers of would-be followers left him. Jesus turned to the inner circle and asked if they would leave too. Peter replied, "Lord, to whom shall we go? You have the words of eternal life" (John 6:68). I for one believe that answer to be profoundly true.

2. The New Testament also claims that God raised Jesus from the dead. If this is true, we are yet again forced to the conclusion that God is active in our world. So once again, what appears to be a vast theoretical question about the existence of God, is in reality a historical problem. A problem about making sense of Jesus, and of the way in which Christianity began.

If the evidence outlined in Chapter 16 is correct, we have our answer. God does exist. We know this because he sent his Son to us, and his Son gave his life for us. When men crucified him, God raised him from the dead. This is the central Christian claim, and pages 125–163 form the core of this book.

In addition to pointing to God's existence, the resurrection highlights aspects of his character: he is the source of Life, of Joy, and of wonderful surprises.

In the light of this, the fact that we find design in the universe takes on a new significance. We may not believe in God *because* of design. But if we believe in God because of Jesus Christ, then we learn that the harmony and pattern is, after all, due to God.

Feel the firm earth under your feet. Ponder the fact that it is moving in orbit round the sun at about 100,000 kilometres per hour. Look at the heavens, and remember that light from the nearest star takes over four years to reach earth – and light travels at 186,282 miles per second.

Enjoy the scent, colour and intricacy of a delicate flower. Consider the beautiful simplicity of the recurring pattern of the seasons. Contemplate the fact that underlying it all is a complexity so great, that the world's scientists constantly need to review and revise their findings.

The God who cares for us; the God who came to us; the God with whom we can communicate in prayer; the God who will give to our lives both meaning and power, if we will allow him – he it is who designed, and who created, and who upholds, all things.

If we can be moved by anything, this will move us. With the Psalmist we will declare:

Great is the Lord and most worthy of praise; his greatness
  no one can fathom.
One generation will commend your works to another;
  they will tell of your mighty acts (Psalm 145: 3–4)

CONCLUDING QUOTATIONS

God has shown us in the life, death and resurrection of Jesus
Christ that divine love is at the heart of the universe, and that
when we live according to that love we will understand what
the universe is about – *Dr. Donald English*.

There is no easy way of describing the reality of God. But
maybe that is just the point: we do not understand him, but we
can recognise him in the face of Jesus, in the depths of our own
hearts, in the experience of wonder. And we know him in
worship, trust and obedience – *Dr. John Habgood, Archbishop
of York*.

TAKE A BREAK (7)
RATHER MORE SERIOUS

The story is told of a man who walked too near the edge of a
cliff. He fell off, and as he plunged down, he put out his hand
and hung on to a thorn bush growing from the cliff face. He
looked up: the cliff was too high to climb. He looked down: it
was far too far to fall!

In desperation he looked up again and shouted, "Is there
anyone there?" To his delight, there was an answering voice.
"Yes, I – the Lord your God – am here." "What shall I do?"
called the man. After a pause, the voice replied, "Let go." The
man looked down at the rocks 100 metres below. Then he
looked up, and called out again, "Is there anyone *else* there?"

*   *   *

This final *Take a Break* has a sting in the tail. I suggest that *we*
are rather like the man on the cliff. We look at the world around
us – at its beauty, and at its chaos – and we wonder, "Is there
anyone there?"

We receive our answer. "Yes, *I* am here: the Lord your God, revealed in Jesus Christ."

Like the man in the story, we are alarmed. For this is not the God we want. *This* God makes tough demands. He tells us that we must deny ourselves; that we must take up a cross, and follow Jesus. He insists that we cannot – must not – live for ourselves; that I *am* my brother's keeper. He calls us to a life of faith – insisting that we stop trusting in perishable things (our savings, our health, our work . . .) and trust in him alone.

Like the man on the cliff, we do not like what we hear. So we call out again: "Is there anyone *else* there?" But there isn't. It is *this* God, or no God at all.

Unlike the man on the cliff we have good reason to heed that voice. Above all, we have the promise of Jesus who said: "Do not be afraid, little flock, for your Father has been pleased to give you the kingdom" (Luke 12:32).

This is the message of the Bible. It brings deep comfort. It also carries strong demands. The main thrust of its message is all too clear. Mark Twain spoke for most of us when he said that it wasn't the parts of Scripture that he *didn't* understand that worried him. It was the parts that he *did* understand that were the trouble!

Of course there is an easy way out of Mark Twain's dilemma. I once heard of a man who was very disturbed when he kept reading about the connection between smoking and lung cancer. So he resolved there and then to give up. He stuck to his resolve, and throughout his short life, he never touched a book again.

21

The Case Against Inertia

It is my conviction that "The Case Against Christ" is not strong. The evidence *for* him is very strong indeed.

It is vitally important to keep the discussion about Christianity centred on this question of evidence.

"His hobby is gardening. My hobby is fishing. Your hobby is religion." Such an attitude is common but inadequate. Christianity just won't fit into a list of hobbies or interests. It is far too big for that.

People follow Jesus for a variety of reasons. Some, because they have a keen sense of sin and know that they need forgiveness and moral power. Some because they feel inadequate to deal with life, and know that they need help. Others because they are deeply impressed by the life of a particular Christian or group of Christians. Yet others because they read the New Testament and are convinced that Jesus Christ is the Son of God.

All these are valid reasons. But the *primary* reason for

becoming a Christian, which underlies them all, is that *Christianity is true*.

A personal note will be appropriate here. The *basic* reason why I am a Christian is not because I have a religious temperament (I'm not sure that I have); nor because I find it convenient (its moral teaching is often extremely *in*convenient); nor because it brings comfort (although it does); nor even because I find in it the strength which I need to live my daily life (although I do).

I am a Christian because I am convinced that the Christian Faith is *true*.

I am persuaded that the Jesus of the Gospels rings true. I am further persuaded that in him, love and hatred, light and darkness, life and death have contended – and that he is Victor, Lord and King.

If anyone could show me that Christianity is not true, then I would have nothing more to do with it.

We are not dealing with a matter of personal taste, but with a question of truth or falsehood. Either Jesus *is* the Son of God, or he is not. Either he *did* rise from the dead or he did not. Either he *is* alive and able to help us today, or he is not.

But in my experience, most people do not apply the test of truth. Instead they are influenced by the spirit of the age, by the opinions of family and friends, and by the widespread indifference to Christianity. The words of G. K. Chesterton continue to be true: "The Christian ideal has not been tried and found wanting. It has been found difficult; and left untried."

Practical: The fact that the central question concerns truth and straight thinking does not mean that Christianity is mere theory – and so without practical implications.

A few years ago I discovered that a woman in a crinoline probably introduced overarm bowling into cricket (try bowling in one and you will see why!). It is perfectly appropriate to follow such a discovery with the comment, "How interesting." Other discoveries – that your house is on fire, or that you have inherited a fortune – must be followed by positive action.

The discovery that Christianity is true comes into the second category.

To accept Jesus because he is the Truth involves a revolution in our behaviour and moral standards, and in our entire outlook on life – for he comes with tough demands.

He comes, too, with unutterable comfort. To a world beset by problems he comes as guide. In a world where many are lonely, he comes as friend. To a world which often seems to lack meaning, he brings understanding. For a world tempted to despair, he provides the ground of hope. Over a world where dying is the single certainty, he sits enthroned as the conqueror of death.

The words of Jesus, as recorded by St. John, have been tested and proved in the lives of countless thousands of men and women: "I am the light of the world. Whoever follows me will never walk in darkness, but will have the light of life" (John 8:12).

22

Postscript: Where Now?

One reader of the typescript suggested that I should write a final note for those readers who want to turn vague good intentions into decisive action. He had in mind those readers who are convinced that Jesus Christ is the Light and Saviour of the world – and those who are uncertain, but keen to keep the enquiry going. With such people in mind I would like to highlight four universal needs.

1. *We all need inspiration, direction and challenge.* So I want to encourage you to read the Bible – and especially the Gospels, where you can meditate on the life and teaching of Jesus. I suggest that you start with St. Mark, then read a few of the New Testament letters. A modern translation makes the text much clearer.

2. *We all need friendship* – one good reason for going to church. In addition to finding friendship you will learn more about the Christian Faith through sermons, and more about the Christian family through experiencing its love – and its faults!

3. *We all need forgiveness and strength.* So we need to pray. "Lord, have mercy on me, a sinner" is a good prayer to start with. Other people need help too. One way of loving them is to pray for them.

4. *We all need markers in our lives.* It often helps to make a definite move. So if you are clear that you want to launch out on the Christian life, or if you want to recommit yourself to

Christ, I suggest that you take a piece of paper and write on it
something like "On this day . . . I make a Covenant with God.
Signed . . ." On the same piece of paper you might care to write
out a prayer or a Bible verse. If you decide to do this, I suggest
that you do two further things. Lend this book to a friend, as a
small act of Christian witness. And write to me c/o Religious
Books, Hodder Headline plc, 338 Euston Road, London NW1
3BH – for I should like to pray for you.

*   *   *

Grace and peace be yours in abundance through the knowledge of God and of Jesus our Lord (2 Pet. 1:2)

23

Suggestions for Group Discussion

INTRODUCTORY NOTES

Several groups have used *The Case Against Christ* for study
and discussion purposes, and it has formed the basis of two
local BBC radio Lent courses. So it seems sensible to give some
guidance to other groups wanting to tackle the subjects
contained in this book.

One encouraging aspect of today's church is the growing
number of small groups meeting in homes and elsewhere.
Such groups often express the need for written material and
these notes are intended as a stimulus to discussion. Each
group has a life of its own and I don't imagine – or intend –
that every group will work methodically through every
question. These notes are meant as a launching pad. Their
sole purpose is to get you thinking, talking and praying.
Please pick and choose; what follows should be a flexible
resource.

You will, I hope, find it helpful to read the relevant pages in
the book itself, before or after your meetings, but increased
head knowledge is only one outcome of lively group discussion. Another important purpose is to gain the courage to share
our faith, our doubts, our fears, our joys, our questions and our
uncertainties. Also, of course, as we listen to other members
and seek to express our own views, we get a firmer grasp of the
important issues we are considering.

In this discussion guide I haven't adopted a chapter-by-
chapter approach. To ask you to live with this book for twenty-
two weeks would be a sure way of killing interest! If you get

seven or eight weeks of lively discussion from this material, I shall be well pleased.

You may wish to use the following prayers to start and end your time together.

Scripture sentence and opening prayer

Jesus said, "*I am the light of the world. Whoever follows me will never walk in darkness, but will have the light of life*" (John 8:12).

Lord of light, please shed your light into our lives. As we talk together, give us the humility to listen, the boldness to speak and the courage to allow your Spirit to challenge and change us. Grant that we may be used to shine your light into our often dark world. Amen.

Scripture sentence and closing prayer

Jesus said, "*If anyone chooses to do God's will, he will find out whether my teaching comes from God*" (John 7:17).

Lord of life, please give us the courage and strength to apply to our lives what we have learned. By your Spirit, help us to see you more clearly, follow you more nearly and love you more dearly, day by day. Amen.

SESSION 1   FAITH, CHURCH AND SINCERITY

• You may find it helpful to use the prayers on page 193.

Sincerity

1.   As a group, draw up a list of sincerely held beliefs which are, in your view, false. (For example, my list would include a) horoscopes and b) the notion that long prison sentences will reduce crime.) Then read and discuss the section which starts on page 25.

Religion is dull

2.   Jean Vanier said: "We all have to choose between two ways of being crazy: the foolishness of the Gospel and the nonsense of the values of our world" (see page 49). Perhaps people think that Christianity is dull because we believers are dull! We rejoice when God tames a wild person (see page 173); perhaps we should rejoice even more when God makes tame people a bit more "wild".

Please tick a box.

I am by nature:

a) A very cautious person   ☐   c) A very daring person   ☐
b) A fairly cautious person ☐   d) A fairly daring person ☐
                e) Other description . . . .

You might share your ticks and see if others agree with your insights into yourself. Comments under "Other description" might be particularly interesting!

• If you ticked a) or b) can you think of an area of your life where God wants your faith to make you more adventurous?
• If you ticked c) or d) can you think of an area of your life where God wants your faith to make you more cautious or controlled?
• Do we use church to shelter from the world outside? Is this

wrong?
- What do you make of Jean Vanier's statement? (see footnote on page 49).

3. Some people accuse the Church of being boring, while others feel that many churches have gone too far in attempting to correct this image – laughter and clapping in church are now common.

- What do you feel about this?
- If you had a free hand, what alterations (if any) would you make to services in your church?
- No grumbling behind backs, please! How can you pass on this information to church leaders?
- What do you make of James' injunction to "grieve, mourn and wail" (Jas. 4:9)? (See page 32.)

Wishful thinking and superstition

4. How would you respond to the accusation that your faith is:
   a) wishful thinking, i.e. that you are afraid to face the reality that there is no God and death is the end? (See page 28.)
   b) nothing but superstition?

Church and faith

5. "You don't need to go to church to be a Christian." Well, do you?

6. Archbishop Michael Ramsey suggested that participating in worship should transform us into channels for God's love and power (page 30).

- If an outsider were to ask how *you* and *your church* shed God's love and power into your neighbourhood, would you be tongue-tied or could you respond with confidence? How can you improve the situation?

7. Do you know people whose lives have been transformed

by Christ (examples are scattered throughout the book, e.g. pages 27 and 181)? Describe them to the group. Include yourself if this is relevant.

8.   As plain George Thomas, Lord Tonypandy was a respected Speaker of the House of Commons – and a popular Methodist lay preacher. His political ability and his Christian faith were tested severely during the Aberfan disaster of 1966. 116 children and 26 adults were tragically killed when a mountain of coal and dust engulfed the town on 21st October. As Government Minister for Wales, George visited every home which had suffered bereavement. Recently he suffered from cancer (of the throat) and he summed up his faith like this: "My Christian faith is the spur to my every endeavour and my source of strength in trouble."

• How does your faith relate to that statement? Could you honestly say that?

9.   You may wish to discuss *Words Worth Weighing* below.
10.   Start next week's questions if you have time to spare.

Note: If you wish to view interviews on video, in which the Archbishop of York, Roy and Fiona Castle, Lord Tonypandy (George Thomas) and others speak about their faith, see page 223.

WORDS WORTH WEIGHING

Holiness involves friendship with God. God's love for us and ours for him grows like any relationship with other people. There comes a moment, which we can never quite locate or catch, when an acquaintance becomes a friend. In a sense, the change from one to the other has been taking place over a period of time, but there comes a point when we know we can trust the other, exchange confidences, keep each other's secrets. We are friends. There has to be a moment like that in our relationship with God. He ceases to be just a Sunday acquaintance and becomes a weekday friend – *Cardinal Basil Hume*.

SESSION 2   CHRISTIANITY IN THE MODERN WORLD

● You may find it helpful to use the prayers on page 193.

1. ● Jot down a short list of problems which keep people whom you know from becoming disciples of Jesus. Share with the group and compare findings.
   ● Jot down a list of problems which trouble you (or troubled you in the past) about the Christian faith. Share with the group and compare findings.

2. The Bible often speaks about the inspiration we can draw from other people who live the life of faith (e.g. Heb. 11). Have you been privileged to meet, or read about, people or organisations whose faith and love have helped you? Describe them to the group.

3. "My friend is an atheist and a communist – but he's as good a Christian as you or me." "It is boasting to call yourself a Christian."

● In view of widespread confusion, how would you define the word "Christian"? (Pages 36–39 and 40 might help.)
● If someone asked you:
   a) "Why should I become a Christian?"
   b) "How can I become a Christian?"
   what would you say?

4. Roy Castle is a popular T.V. personality. Life was good when, out of the blue, he fell seriously ill with lung cancer. This experience strengthened his faith and the already strong faith of Fiona, his wife. In fact, Roy had come to Christian faith gradually over a period of time, before his illness. For years he had been aware of "holding the hand of God" as he went through life – but his head was down. One day he looked up and saw the face of God revealed in Jesus Christ.

   Roy's journey to faith was gradual although it eventually came to a clear focus. Others (e.g. Fred Lemon, see page 173) were catapulted into faith rather like St. Paul.

- Members of the group are invited to share the outlines of their own spiritual pilgrimages. Were there key people, organisations or experiences? Did faith come suddenly or gradually (see *Words Worth Weighing*)?

5. Read the postscripts on meaning (page 21) brainwashing (page 34) and on sin and guilt (page 39). Are there any points which you disagree with, or strongly endorse?

6. The New Testament uses many words/phrases to describe the followers of Jesus.

- Brainstorm your group to see how many of these words/phrases you can recall. The following Bible references might fill in the gaps. Matt. 5:13; Matt. 5:14; John 13: 34,35; Acts 1:8; Acts 5:14; Acts 11:26; 1 Cor. 6:19; Eph.1:1; 2 Tim. 2:3; Philem. 16; 1 Pet. 2:11.
- Each title throws light upon a different aspect of the Christian life. Ponder and discuss these descriptions and their significance.

7. Read the words of Lord Rees-Mogg on page 51.

- Do you agree with him?
- Does his comment have any practical relevance for you and me?
- Do his comments apply only to famous "official" saints, or can we ordinary believers play a part in "saving the world"? How?

8. Bishop Lesslie Newbigin is a leading Christian of our century. He has wide experience of the world church and spent many years as a missionary in South India. On returning to England he observed that modern Britain is the toughest mission field in which he has worked. He spoke of encountering "cold contempt" for the Gospel. Some British Christians might be tempted to envy Lesslie Newbigin, for they do not encounter hostility. Instead, they find that the case against Christ (or *for him*) is simply ignored.

- Do you encounter indifference or hostility to your faith?
- What might you do in the face of this? (For *80 Practical Suggestions for a Decade of Evangelism* write to St. Paul's Church Office (CAC), Holgate Road, York, YO2 4BB. Please enclose £1 in stamps.)

WORDS WORTH WEIGHING

That is why everyone is challenged to respond to God through Jesus Christ in a personal turning (which is what the word "conversion" means). You have to meet Jesus yourself, and to accept him as your friend and as your Lord. In many Christian lives, this turning or conversion reaches a climax which can be dated. But it is not necessary to be able to date your conversion like that.

What is essential is that everyone should have his or her personal reasons for being a Christian. You cannot inherit Christian faith as you can inherit red hair or a peculiar nose. You cannot copy Christian faith as you can copy a hairstyle or an accent. And you cannot get it completely out of books, as you can get a knowledge of history. Your faith, to be authentic, to guide your life, must be your own. Your very own experience, whether it is dramatic or quiet, long or short, must lead you to know Jesus Christ as your personal Liberator – *David L. Edwards*.

SESSION 3   SCIENCE AND CHRISTIAN FAITH

- You may wish to use the prayers on page 193.

1.   Personal

- I enjoy good health, but without modern medical science I should be deaf (ear wax), lame (foot fungus) and toothless (general decay). Describe *yourselves* in a non-scientific age (if you dare!).
- List *two or three other benefits* of modern science. Share your ideas with the group. Do you ever thank God for these advances? Should you?
- List *two or three problems* (ethical or practical) caused by modern science. Share with the group. Do you ever pray about these problems? Should you?

2.   General

Popular interest in science is strong. Recently I visited the Science Museum in Boston USA, which was full of people enjoying the "hands on" approach. At a more literary level we note the fact that Stephen Hawking's *A Brief History of Time* remained at the top of the bestseller list for a record number of months. No doubt this is partly due to interest in a remarkable person. Just *how does* he achieve so much, given his multiple handicaps? But it also indicates the continuing hold of science on the popular imagination. However:

a) Popular interest in science is linked with concern about the great "God questions", i.e. can we find design and purpose in the universe? Is there a Mind behind its beautiful order? Hawking himself – though not a Christian believer – raises these questions.

b) Some writers on the religion/science interface are very optimistic about science, e.g. Paul Davies asserts in *The New Physics*: "It may seem bizarre but in my opinion science offers a surer path to God than religion".

c) Others see science as more of a threat to humanity than an asset. "It is becoming increasingly evident that the modern gods of the West – science, technology, and industrialisation –

have lost their magic. Events of world history have shaken Western civilisation to the core . . . we are heading for an ecological disaster on a cosmic scale . . . progress was, in effect, a false god" (David J. Bosch). Many questions arise from all this.

- What on earth does Paul Davies mean? Any guesses?
- Do you share the pessimistic view outlined above, or do you believe that scientific progress brings hope? Why?
- Do you know people who believe that science has disproved religion? What would you say to them?
- Are there any other points you wish to raise?

3. Stars and tea leaves

I was crossing London's Victoria Station when I saw a large stall with flashing lights. It was selling "Your Horoscope by Computer". This mixture of technology and superstition is a significant commentary on modern Britain. Science delivers the goods: electricity in our homes, safe drinking water . . . But science doesn't deliver *all* the goods, so we hedge our bets. Instead of turning to a demanding faith like Christianity, modern people take an easy option – horoscopes on T.V. or in the newspaper. So the power of science and technology is neatly combined with a deeply-felt sense that there is "something more" to life than the material world. Together they squeeze out full-blooded Christianity, which demands commitment and discipleship.

- Do you agree/disagree with this summary of British people today?
- Do you ever read your horoscope?
- Many people do, on the grounds that "it's a harmless bit of fun", but many Christians believe that it is (a) foolish and (b) harmful. What do you think?
- "Science – like architecture, education, medicine and theology – is far too important to be left to the experts." Do you agree?
- How can we make the Gospel of Jesus Christ live for our neighbours in our scientific age?

4.　Miracles in a scientific age

John Polkinghorne (a former Professor of Mathematical Physics at Cambridge University) believes that ideas from science can help our Christian imagination – *superconductivity*, for example! Usually it takes energy to "push" electricity through a wire, but if the temperature is lowered sufficiently, the normal laws cease to operate and current passes freely around the circuit without "push" or resistance. Hence "superconductivity". The laws of physics haven't changed, but *because the situation is drastically altered, new consequences come into play* and something un-expected and remarkable happens.

John Polkinghorne suggests that the miracles of Jesus can be understood in this way. In Jesus the "usual state of affairs" was drastically altered, for God became man. Hence the Gospel miracles, and especially the miracle of the Resurrection.

- Do you find these insights helpful, or irrelevant? Should we simply accept Jesus' miracles and not try to understand?
- Do you believe that Jesus performed miracles?
- Do you believe that miracles continue to happen today? (See pages 173–175.) If so, why not more frequently – or always? If so, is God a "celestial conjuror" rather than a heavenly Father?
- Read Mark 2:1–12. Then ask: what significance do Jesus' miracles have for us today?
- Bishop David Jenkins wrote: "For my part I am quite clear that miracles occur . . . but I am equally clear that I do not believe in God because of miracles . . . miracles are not proofs of power but gifts of love to be received by faith." Is this helpful?

5.　Alone in the universe?

Professor Russell Stannard, Professor of Physics and a Christian preacher, says that, given the immensity of the universe, "almost certainly" there is intelligent life on other planets. He adds: "In the same way as the Son of God came to earth and

took on the form of a man – the man Jesus – I see no reason why the same Son of God should not take on other forms for the benefit of life on the other planets."

● Does this worry you, excite you, or . . . ?

Note: An exciting recent development was the announcement in 1993 of the establishment at Cambridge University of the *Starbridge Lectureship in Theology and Natural Science*. Novelist Susan Howatch is funding this (one million pounds!) in order to "strike a blow for theology to show that religion is not dead, but complements scientific discovery".

WORDS WORTH WEIGHING

Scientists have discovered that the laws of nature have to be "finely-tuned" to allow the possibility for life to develop. If the power of gravity, or the charge on the electron, or the nature of nuclear forces, were even a little different from what they actually are, no life could have come into being. The distinguished theoretical physicist Freeman Dyson wrote that, "The more I examine the universe and the details of its architecture, the more evidence I find that the universe in some sense must have known that we were coming" – *John Polkinghorne*.

SESSION 4   MORE ON CHRISTIANITY AND SCIENCE

- You may wish to use the prayers on page 193.

1.   Prayer in a scientific age

Science used to present a mechanistic view of the universe. It was thought that everything runs like clockwork, so the power of prayer and the possibility of miracles were easily excluded. Today, science presents a more complex picture: packets of energy; huge empty spaces; a principle of uncertainty; a large degree of chance at the sub-atomic "micro-level"; systems so complicated that their behaviour can *never* be predicted. In an open, flexible world like this, perhaps the power of prayer and the God of miracles fit rather more comfortably?

Not everyone agrees, of course. Bill's son was ill and I said I would pray. "Don't bother," said Bill, "I'm putting my faith in the doctors, not God." His response was unusual – most people are glad to know that people are praying for them. When his son George had leukaemia, Gary Lineker said he was grateful to all the people who were praying for his family.

- Which response (Bill's or Gary's) is more common, in your experience? Can you give further examples?
- The healing ministry of the Church, and the task of praying for sick people, play an important role in the life of many churches. Do you believe that such prayers are effective?
- Do you have personal experience of specific answers to prayer?
- Are these the right questions to ask? Does it matter whether or not we can point to "obvious" answers to our prayers?
- If you are interested in a church outreach scheme ("prayer visiting") based on the fact that most people believe in prayer, write for the booklet on page 199.

Note: Pages 174–178 address some of these questions, e.g. the experience of Irina Ratushinskaya. While enduring freezing conditions in a Soviet labour camp, she felt physical and emotional warmth for no obvious reason. She believes that this was because people were praying for her (see page 178). Was this self delusion or deep sanity?

Trappist monk Thomas Merton went even further. He believed that prayer prevents the world from "cracking apart" and being engulfed in darkness and chaos. This relates to St. Paul's teaching about "spiritual warfare" (Eph. 6). Much food for thought! (And for discussion?)

2. Light

Turn to page 75 and read the top three paragraphs.
- Does this express the way you feel about life?
- Do you feel that such an approach is practical and helpful – or too "fuzzy"?

3. Genesis

In the light of scientific explanations of the origins of life, is the book of Genesis a problem for you? With which of the three approaches to the accounts of the Creation in the Bible are you most comfortable? (See pages 60–64.)

4. The heart of the matter

Pages 66–69 take us to the heart of the relationship between science and Christianity.

- Do you find the examples convincing?
- Can you add others?

5. The human sciences

The great psychologist Carl Gustav Jung said: "During the past thirty years people from all the civilised countries of the earth have consulted me . . . Among my patients in the second half of life – that is to say over thirty-five – there has not been one whose problem in the last resort was not that of finding a religious outlook on life".

- How does that relate to your knowledge of other people – and yourself?

6. The parable of the mice

Does the mice parable (page 77) "work", i.e. does it make a valid point in a valid way? Some people feel that it is too "clever". By leaving the reader on a sad note it seems to be denying a Creator (not my intention!). Is this criticism valid?

7. Design in the universe

Writing in *The Times* (14.4.91) Clifford Longley argued that the "just right" factor points to God as Designer:

> The anthropic principle is the most intriguing new scientific idea of the last decade . . . It is a massive piece of circumstantial evidence pointing to meaning and purpose in the universe . . . The precise values of the speed of light, Planck's Constant, the mass of protons compared with neutrons, the total quantity of hydrogen and helium – all apparently unconnected conditions which have controlled every detail of the universe's development – seem to have been exactly programmed at or just after the first moment of time, and all to one end: humanity. Any deviation (and the odds on such deviations were tremendous) would have made the development of the universe as you know it, life included, impossible . . . If in the course of an experiment a scientist produced a result against odds this large, he certainly would not dismiss it as an accident. He would look for a cause.

Read, too, *Words Worth Weighing* on page 203.

- Do the facts of pattern, order, beauty and remarkable "coincidences" which gave rise to life, convince you that there is a Designer?
- What about ugliness and destruction? (See pages 113–122.)
- Can science ever prove or disprove the existence of God?
- Do you find the following comment from R. T. France in *The Living God* convincing?

It boils down to this: you cannot expect an atheist to reach a personal knowledge of God through looking at nature; but you can expect a Christian's observation of nature to lead him to worship with greater understanding and reverence the God who has revealed Himself to him.

WORDS WORTH WEIGHING

It is indeed a sobering thought that the early writings of the Jewish people (i.e. our Old Testament) encompass all the basic recommendations of World Conservation strategy – *Professor David Bellamy*.

Note: One sympathetic reader pointed out (page 170) that chance does not rule out design, i.e. scientists are comfortable with words like "random" and "chance" at a micro-level (in the behaviour of sub-atomic particles). In response I would point out that this does not rule out predictable behaviour in the everyday world, i.e. the laws of physics continue to operate. They do so *because* a lot of random happenings can add up to an orderly pattern. This is how life insurance works. Insurance companies do not know when you are doing to die, but if they insure enough people like you, the expected pattern of mortality will enable them to make money.

My friend's criticism shows we use the word "chance" in two senses. When I spoke of chance, I was referring to something much bigger – the possibility of a "designer-less" universe which just happens to "work" and to produce moral, thinking beings, who can appreciate its beauty. You may wish to discuss this (on the other hand, you may not!).

If you wish to read further, I recommend the books mentioned on pages 19 and 64.

SESSION 5   THE BIBLE

- You may wish to spend more than one week on this material.
- You may wish to use the prayers on page 193.

1.   Imagine that a friend is in hospital facing a serious operation. She is interested in, but not sure about, the Christian faith. You suggest that she might read the Bible and she agrees. Which passages would you select?

2.   A non-Christian friend asks you to point to:
   a)   a passage which means a lot to you. Which would you choose and why?
   b)   a word, phrase or Bible passage which "sums up" the message of the whole Bible. Which would you choose?

3.   Imagine that you are in conversation with a new Christian who asks your advice about methods for regular Bible study. What would you say?

4.   A Sikh neighbour asks you to outline:
   a)   the good news or Gospel contained in the Bible. (See *Words Worth Weighing* for a summary by Archbishop Desmond Tutu.)
   b)   the story of the Bible from Genesis to Revelation. Could you? Try it out in pairs in your group.

5.   Imagine that you are a member of one of those early communities of faith (Jewish and Christian) discussing which books should be included in the Bible as Holy Scripture. Most books justify themselves by their ring of truth and authority, but how would you justify:
   a)   an erotic book (Song of Songs)?
   b)   an agnostic book (Ecclesiastes)?
   c)   an anonymous letter (Hebrews)?

6.   Which Bible passages do you have difficulty with, in the light of Mark Twain's quip: "It's not the parts of Scripture that I *don't* understand that worry me; it's the parts that I *do* understand"?

7. In some churches, Bible readings are followed with the declaration, "This is the Word of the Lord". Some Christians feel that this is not always appropriate, e.g. following violent passages like Psalm 137, or "false" passages like Job's comforters. What are your views on this?

8. David L. Edwards writes in *What Anglicans Believe*:

Normally we read as quickly as possible, because we are reading newspapers, light fiction, etc. Or, when we are studying a subject, we read as critically as possible. For a change, try reading suitable parts of the Bible as lovingly as possible, lingering over the scene, noticing every detail as if you had been there, asking what it shows you of God. Such "meditation" on the Bible supplies a solid basis for prayer – and life. When you have got clearer in your mind the reality of God, coming to you in Jesus, stepping out of the pages of the Bible, you will find it easier to put together the jigsaw puzzle of your life.

- Ask a member of your group to read (slowly) a passage from one of the Gospels (perhaps Matt. 8:1–13). Other members of the group might listen with eyes closed to shut out distractions and embarrassment. Keep silence together and enter into the situation in your imagination and try to apply it to your life and circumstances. You may – or may not – wish to share your thoughts.

9. Ask one or two volunteers to summarise pages 83–86 which describe some of the reasons for trusting the New Testament. They may wish to use the diagram on page 210 to assist them.

10. Re-read the remarkable discovery of the Indian mathematician (page 133) and its application to the Gospel story.

- Do you agree with my assessment? To assist your discussion you may wish to re-read pages 87–92 where I suggest that four questions take us to the heart of the big question, "Are the gospels reliable?"

  a) *Could* the writers have invented the material?
  b) *Would* the writers have invented the material?
  c) Do the gospels ring true today?
  d) Can we check any of the details?

WORDS WORTH WEIGHING

What a tremendous relief . . . to discover that we don't need to prove ourselves to God. This is what Jesus came to say, and for that he got killed . . . The Good News is that God loved me long before I could have done anything to deserve it. He is like the father of the prodigal son, waiting anxiously for the return of his wayward son . . . That is tremendous stuff – that is the Good News. Whilst we were yet sinners, says St. Paul, Christ died for us. God did not wait until we were die-able, for He could have waited until the cows came home – *Archbishop Desmond Tutu.*

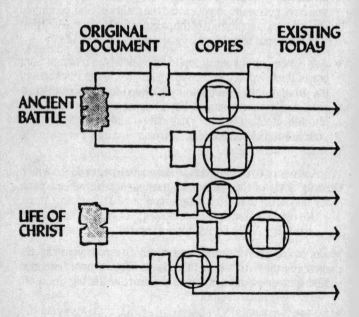

SESSION 6   WHY DOES GOD ALLOW SUFFERING?

- You may wish to spend more than one week on this material.
- You may wish to use the prayers on page 193.

1.   Suffering and faith

Sometimes suffering leads to a loss of faith. On occasions it just
withers and dies; on other occasions, it is rejected with considerable energy. On hearing of the death of his wife in hospital,
one man hit a nurse – because medicine had failed them. He then
went to the chapel and bent the large processional cross –
because God had failed them. *In contrast*, another man came to
faith in Christ following the cot death of his baby.

- Do you know anyone who has turned away from God as a
  result of suffering?
- Do you know anyone whose faith in God has been strengthened as a result of suffering?

Please share this information and keep a confidential list of
names to pray for at the end of the meeting.

2.   Personal suffering

Members of your group are invited to describe their own tough
experiences – and to share how these experiences relate to their
trust in God. Did these times strengthen faith, shake faith
or . . . ?

3.   Inspiration from the Cross

"Jesus is no mere spectator of the anguish of the world. He
understands it *from the inside*. He is able to enter into our
suffering, because he too suffered" (see page 121).

- Do you agree with my reasons (page 121) for not buying the
  Russian picture?
- Do the sufferings of Jesus help you in times of trouble – or
  does the Cross seem a remote event?

4. Strength from the Spirit

Sometimes people feel that God is distant and remote from their pain, but it is also quite common for people to say that they experience God's strength in a fresh way at such times. Can you comment on such an experience – yours, or other people's?

5. Teaching from the Scriptures

An eternal perspective: Read 1 Pet. 1: 6–9. How would you respond to the jibe that this is "pie in the sky when you die"?

Grumbling at God: Read Ps. 10:1 and 13:1. Is it healthy – or irreverent – to bring such an honest complaint directly to God? Is this a helpful model for our prayers? Before leaving this question, please read the *whole* of Psalm 13.

Sharing experience: We can learn a lot about attitudes to suffering from Paul's second letter to the Corinthians. He openly admits that he experienced "conflicts on the outside, fears within" (2 Cor. 7:5).

- What good can come out of suffering? Read 2 Cor. 1:3–4; 1:8–11; 4:16–18; 12:7–10.
- What can we learn about prayer from these verses?
- How did God comfort Paul (7:5–7)?
- Note the way in which Paul thinks of God in 2 Cor. 1:3–4. You may wish to commit these verses to memory.
- Relate your own experience to these verses.

6. What is faith?

Read aloud John Paton's letter from the mission field (page 120) and the more recent comments of Professor Sir Norman Anderson when his twenty-one-year-old son died of cancer (page 122). At the end of John Paton's letter, I comment:

> This is the authentic voice of faith. The person with a living faith is often bewildered, but he is prepared to live with

questions which he cannot answer, in the light of the great answers which he *does* possess.

Such faith is not a blind refusal to face the facts. Rather, it comes from a concern to take into account *all* the facts: the fact of suffering *and* the fact of Christ. Such faith is not based on a refusal to consider the evidence. Indeed it springs from a refusal to leave out that part of the evidence which non-Christians so often ignore – the evidence of God's love shown by the fact that he sent his Son and that he continues to strengthen us by his Spirit.

● Do you find this definition of faith

accurate?   Yes/no   *misleading?*   Yes/no
helpful?   Yes/no   *or?* . . .

● How would **you** define faith?

7. Further thoughts on faith

Cardinal Newman wrote:

> Therefore I will trust him, whatever, wherever I am. I can never be thrown away. If I am in sickness, my sickness may serve him; in perplexity, my perplexity may serve him; if I am in sorrow, my sorrow may serve him. He does nothing in vain. He knows what it is about. He may take away my friends. He may throw me among strangers. He may make me feel desolate, make my spirits sink, hide my future from me – still he knows what he is about.

● In your view is that inspiring truth *or* escapist nonsense *or* . . . ?

8. Suffering and prayer

If you were in trouble would you:
     a)   ask friends to pray for you – or with you?
     b)   be glad to know that the local church was praying?
     c)   prefer to suffer silently and privately?

9. Suffering and miracles

I have heard some Christians claim that all suffering is contrary to God's will. If we pray in faith, God *will* heal. If he doesn't, there's something wrong with our faith. What do you think about this? (See pages 176–178.)

Discuss Question 1 in Session 5 if you have not already done so.

WORDS WORTH WEIGHING

Gerald Priestland was a distinguished Foreign Affairs correspondent with the BBC before becoming Religious Affairs correspondent. He was a Quaker who lived with questions and doubts. In June 1989 he suffered a severe stroke and it was through this that he found the assurance which he lacked before. Shortly before his death in 1991 he wrote: "I have had the feeling of being crushed under a rock till I could see only one crack of light, and that was the love of God, the absolute certainty, when everything else had been taken from me, that God loved me."

BOOKS WORTH READING

The following books relate to the problem of suffering:

Matthew	Bob Jackson (Highland)
Give Us This Day	Fiona Castle (Kingsway)
Joni	Joni Eareckson Tada (Marshall Pickering)

SESSION 7   JESUS

- You may wish to spend more than one week on this material.
- You might find it helpful to use the prayers on page 193.

1.   In the following list, what is Jesus primarily for you? Tick
your answers.

- a figure of history   ...
- a wise teacher   ...
- a loving friend   ...
- a terrifying Judge   ...
- an essential Saviour ...
- *other* . . . .

- a powerful Lord   ...
- a window unto God   ...
- God   ...
- an enigmatic figure   ...
- a beloved brother   ...

Compare your ticks and reasons with other group members.

2.   Read slowly and thoughtfully the statements about Jesus
on pages 123; 130/1 and 145.

- If you had one sentence in which to summarise *your* attitude,
  what would it be?

3.   Do you agree that Jesus' view of himself and his mission leads
inevitably and logically to the assertion by Archbishop Michael
Ramsey that, *"I see no escape from the dilemma: either Jesus is
fraudulent, or his claim is true . . ."*? (See pages 144/5.)

4.   Consider the prayer of St. Richard of Chichester:

  Thanks be to you, my Lord Jesus Christ,
  for all the benefits you have won for us,
  for all the pains and insults you have borne for us.
  Most merciful Redeemer, Friend and Brother,
  may we know you more clearly, love you more dearly,
  and follow you more nearly, day by day. Amen.

Attempt to write your own devotional prayer to Jesus.

5.   It may help to read the whole of Chapter 16 at this point.

● Select for discussion two or three points outlined in Chapter 16 on the resurrection. Do you find them convincing?
● Read the words of Professor C. F. D. Moule on page 160 and ponder the diagram on page 221. Is it possible to answer his question convincingly without coming up with "resurrection"?
● The saintly and scholarly Austin Farrer wrote: "It is possible through faith and evidence together, and through neither alone, to believe that Christ really and corporally rose from the dead." Do you find that helpful?

6.   Mother Teresa of Calcutta said, "Evangelism means to carry Jesus in your heart and to give the presence of Jesus to someone else . . . but to give Jesus to a person you must first have Jesus yourself."

● What does it mean to carry Jesus in your heart?
● What does it mean to give the presence of Jesus to someone else?

7.   Some people would say that their faith in Jesus is a deeply private matter, so evangelism is unwarranted and intrusive. Others would say that to keep the good news about Jesus to ourselves is selfish.

● Where do you stand on this?
● How would you define this good news? (See page 210 for Desmond Tutu's answer.)
● How can it be shared in the modern world? (See address on page 197.)

8.   The implications of the resurrection of Jesus are immense. According to the New Testament, his resurrection is the "first fruit" of a great harvest, so:
    a)   Death is dead
    b)   Jesus is alive – and with us, day by day

- Are these truths immediate and important for you – or distant and abstract?
- Do you have a sense of the risen Christ "accompanying" you through life? (Read the Albert Schweitzer paragraph at the end of this section.)
- David Jenkins, Bishop of Durham from 1984–1994, said that, on dying, he will "fall into the arms of a loving God".
- Do you have a faith like that?
- Do we modern people think too little/too much about "the four last things": death, judgment, heaven and hell?

9. Can you think of an example from your own life or someone else's when you or they were
  a) challenged by Jesus as Teacher and Lord?
  b) encouraged by Jesus as Teacher, Saviour, Friend and Brother?

10. Jesus said some remarkable things. Read the words below and ask: did he intend us to take them literally, or was he pointing us in a certain direction? Group members are asked to describe concrete situations in their own lives, or other people's, when these words have hit home:

- turn the other cheek
- sell your possessions and give to the poor
- if anyone comes after me, he must hate his father and his mother
- forgive seventy times seven
- take no anxious thought for tomorrow
- do not judge, or you will be judged

11. The New Testament makes it clear that Jesus was a real human being. Like us he had emotional highs and lows. Like us he got weary, hungry, thirsty and tired. But that same New Testament makes it clear that Jesus is unique. Even exalted titles like *Prophet* and *Messiah* aren't big enough to contain him. The writers were forced to press language to its limits with terms like *Lord*, *Redeemer*, *Son of God* and *Light of the World*.

There are many more titles for Jesus in the New Testament.

• Brainstorm your group to draw up a list of these.
• Turn to St. John's Gospel and go through quickly, looking for titles for Jesus.
• What do these titles mean for our lives today?

WORDS WORTH WEIGHING

You may wish to read aloud the following affirmations about Jesus, together with others (see Question 2). After this sit quietly, then end the meeting with the prayer of St. Richard of Chichester (Question 4).

He comes to us as one unknown, without a name, as of old by the lakeside he came to those men who knew him not. He speaks to us the same words: "Follow me", and sets us to the tasks which he has to fulfil for our time. He commands. And to those who obey him, whether they be wise or simple, he will reveal himself in the toils, the conflicts, the sufferings which they shall pass through in his fellowship, and they shall learn in their own experience who he is – *Albert Schweitzer*.

When we talk about believing in Jesus, there is a content to it. It's not believing that here was once a nice man who did good things, and who better for an example? That's very thin indeed in terms of New Testament interpretation. It's a person about whom they say: Son of Man, Lord, Saviour, Emmanuel, Word of Life. And every one of those ways of describing him is throbbing with meaning' – *Dr. Donald English*.

SESSION 8   PROVE IT! DOES GOD EXIST?

- You may wish to spend more than one week on this material.
- You might find it helpful to use the prayers on page 193.

I. NO OPTING OUT OF BELIEF

In the modern world, faith is often downgraded. Non-Christians sometimes give the impression that they stand on a firm platform of logic and fact, looking down on lesser mortals who live by faith. In practice:

a) there is no opting out of belief

b) most of the things which *really* matter to us have words like *believe* or *belief* attached to them, e.g. I believe in abortion/I believe that the unborn child should be protected; I believe in freedom of speech, human rights, nursery education for all, fair taxation . . .

- Read and discuss pages 167–168 and these words of Lord Blanch, Archbishop of York, 1975–1983:

When St. Paul said, "The life I now live I live by faith in the Son of God who loved me and gave Himself for me," he was not setting himself apart from the world by virtue of his faith, but only by virtue of Him in whom he put his faith . . . The world is divided therefore not between those who believe and those who do not believe, but between those who believe in the powers of the world and those who believe in the Power of God.

- If you were challenged to explain why you believe in God, what would you say? You may wish to use the questionnaire below, "borrowed" from my book *Know Your Faith*.

I believe in God because:

a) of the beauty around me . . .   f) of what I read in the Bible . . .

b) of harmony in nature   . . .   g) of Jesus Christ   . . .

c) I instinctively "know"   h) of people I have met   . . .
   that he is there   . . .   i) of the church   . . .

d) of a personal experience . . .   j) . . . .

e) of a whole range of
   personal experiences   . . .

- Surveys continue to show that most people in Britain and America believe in God, but there are obvious differences between head belief and active faith.

  a) What are these?
  b) Where do you figure on the following scale:

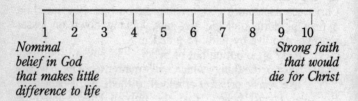

| | | | | | | | | | |
|1|2|3|4|5|6|7|8|9|10|

Nominal belief in God that makes little difference to life

Strong faith that would die for Christ

c) What measures can you take to move up the scale?

II. DOES GOD EXIST?

In the Section entitled *Prove It!* in the main body of the book (page 165 onwards), an argument is developed. It is suggested that three factors come together and point to the existence of a loving God who created and sustains the universe:

1. An orderly universe

This is not put forward as a "knock-down" argument – although some writers believe that it is (see the bold assertion by Clifford Longley on page 206 and *Words Worth Weighing* on page 203). Over and against order, beauty and a whole series of remarkable "coincidences" which have led to life, there is the problem of chaos and destruction.

There are three classic responses to the two sets of appearances (order *and* chaos) presented by our universe. Some say that it points to a Designer: at the heart of the universe we find love, purpose and meaning. Others (atheists) hold that we live in a cold, unfeeling world. In their view, the universe came about by a random series of coincidences. Others (agnostics) maintain that we simply don't have enough evidence to decide either way.

While I do believe (passionately) that we can find love, meaning, truth and God at the centre of our universe – and at the centre of our personal lives – I also believe that the other positions need to be taken seriously. So I have moved on to consider two other vital areas of evidence: history and personal experience.

2. Evidence from history

Considerable space is given to this in the body of the book, especially in the sections on the Bible and on Jesus. Various questions arising from these chapters have already appeared in this discussion guide, so no further questions will be added at this point. Instead we shall concentrate on the third strand of evidence:

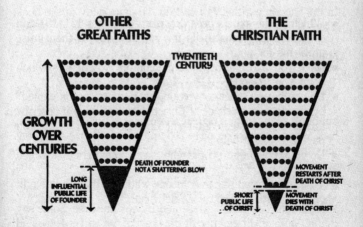

3.　Evidence from personal experience

The experiences noted in Chapter 19 are (I think!) interesting and significant. I would encourage you to re-read the entire chapter.

Quotations and questions

"I am unable to see how a man can find the hand of God in secular history, unless he has first found that he has an assurance of it in his personal experiences" (Herbert Butterfield).

"Unlike science, where an experiment can be observed . . . you must do the experiment (of faith) for yourself" (Russell Stannard).

"Science must admit the psychological validity of religious experience" (Sir William Cecil Dampier).

"I came to know God experimentally" (George Fox).

- Which of the experiences described on pages 171–181 and elsewhere ring most bells for you? Do any of them raise problems for you?
- Have you had one or more memorable experiences which point you to God?
- Do you have a quiet conviction that you are "accompanied" by the unseen presence of Christ? How would you describe this to an interested enquirer? (Albert Schweitzer's words on page 218 might help).
- Do you know other people who have had experiences which point them to God?
- What would you say to someone who said that all this talk of experience of God is self-delusion?

III. THE CASE AGAINST INERTIA

"If you believe what you like in the Gospel and reject what you like, it is not the Gospel you believe, but yourself" (St. Augustine).

"By dying like that, Jesus has won the right to be 'our Lord'. The word 'Lord' here means 'boss'" (David L. Edwards).

"Christianity is a statement which, if false, is of no importance, and if true, of infinite importance. The one thing it cannot be is moderately important" (C. S. Lewis).

- Do you sometimes feel that *in practice* you relegate your faith to a position of "moderate importance"? Be practical and specific – and as honest as you dare! Reflect upon your use of time, money, energy, gifts, etc.
- A little girl fell out of bed and sobbed: "I think I stayed too near to where I got in, Mummy!" Could that describe your Christian journey?
- Invite one member of the group to read page 188 out loud. Turn these words into prayer or invite each member to write a prayer based on the challenge and comfort of Christ. Close by using these prayers.
- You may wish to tackle neglected questions from earlier chapters.

Notes
1. If you wish to borrow a video which contains interviews with Roy and Fiona Castle, Lord Tonypandy, the Archbishop of York, and other less famous Christians, write to The One Voice Office (CAC), St. Paul's Church, Holgate Road, York, YO2 4BB. Please enclose £1.50 in stamps for postage and packing.

2. If you want further material for group discussion you might:

   - try other books listed on page 2.
   - Turn over – for comments on *Know Your Faith*.

KNOW YOUR FAITH

by

John Young

The excitement of Christian truth presented afresh in an eight-week study of the Apostles' Creed.

"I am delighted to commend John Young's book warmly. *Know Your Faith* will be a major resource for parish groups and individuals."

George Carey, Archbishop of Canterbury

"Anyone who sits in on a group which follows these eight investigations into the Apostles' Creed (or, better still, spends sixteen sessions on them, for they contain so much good material) will end up as a more informed and more intelligent Christian than when they began."

John Taylor, Bishop of St. Albans

"John Young has a great gift for communicating profound ideas simply and readably. His skills were never more needed as the churches launch into the Decade of Evangelism."

John Habgood, Archbishop of York

This book is designed for individual readers and for discussion groups.